EDITOR: Maryanne Blacker

DESIGN DIRECTOR: Neil Carlyle

FOOD EDITOR: Pamela Clark

▪ ▪ ▪

DESIGNER: Paula Wooller

▪ ▪ ▪

DEPUTY FOOD EDITOR: Jan Castorina

ASSISTANT FOOD EDITOR: Kathy Snowball

ASSOCIATE FOOD EDITOR:
Enid Morrison

SENIOR HOME ECONOMISTS: Jill Lange,
Louise Patniotis, Kathy Wharton

HOME ECONOMISTS: Tracey Kern, Quinton Kohler,
Alexandra McCowan, Kathy McGarry, Andrew Nunn,
Dimitra Stais

EDITORIAL COORDINATOR: Elizabeth Hooper

KITCHEN ASSISTANT: Amy Wong

▪ ▪ ▪

STYLISTS: Lucy Andrews, Rosemary de Santis,
Carolyn Fienberg, Jane Hann, Jacqui Hing

COVER STYLIST: Marie-Helene Clauzon

PHOTOGRAPHERS: Kevin Brown, Robert Clark,
Robert Taylor, Jon Waddy

▪ ▪ ▪

HOME LIBRARY STAFF:

ASSISTANT EDITOR: Judy Newman

DESIGNER: Robbylee Phelan

EDITORIAL COORDINATOR: Lara Quinlin

▪ ▪ ▪

ACP PUBLISHER: Richard Walsh

ACP ASSOCIATE PUBLISHER: Bob Neil

▪ ▪ ▪

Produced by The Australian Women's Weekly Home Library.
Typeset by Letter Perfect, Sydney. Printed by Dai Nippon Co.,
Ltd in Japan. Published by Australian Consolidated Press,
54 Park Street Sydney. ♦ **Australia:** Distributed by Network
Distribution Company, 54 Park Street Sydney, (02) 282 8777.
♦ **New Zealand:** Distributed in New Zealand by Netlink
Distribution Company (9) 302 7616.
♦ **United Kingdom:** Distributed in the U.K. by Australian
Consolidated Press (UK) Ltd, (0604) 760 456.
♦ **Canada:** Distributed in Canada by Whitecap
Books Ltd, (604) 9809852. ё **South Africa:** Distributed in
South Africa by Intermag (011) 4933200.
ACN 000 031 747.

▪ ▪ ▪

The Minced Meat Cookbook

Includes index.
ISBN 0 949128 83 X.

1. Mincemeat. 2. Cookery (Meat).
(Series : Australian Women's Weekly
Home Library).

641.66

▪ ▪ ▪

© A C P 1992
This publication is copyright. No part of it may be reproduced
or transmitted in any form without the written permission
of the publishers.

▪ ▪ ▪

COVER: Clockwise from back: Tabbouleh Meatballs,
page 11, Shepherd's Pie Pots, page 64,
Spiced Beef Pasta Salad, page 60.
China and napkin from Accoutrement.
OPPOSITE: Ground Lamb with Pine Nuts and Witlof,
page 41.
BACK COVER: Nugget Pumpkins with Chicken and Spinach
Sauce, page 95.

THE MINCED MEAT COOKBOOK

It's amazing what we've done with minced meat! Beef, lamb, chicken, and pork and veal are used in more ways than you'd ever have thought possible, with fabulous flavours from around the world to give you a terrific variety of easy recipes. We used top-quality lean mince and we recommend you do the same for best results. It should be finely ground (ask your butcher to grind it again or re-mince in your food processor at home, if necessary). If you prefer, buy and mince the cut of your choice.

Pamela Clark

FOOD EDITOR

BRITISH & NORTH AMERICAN READERS: Please note that Australian cup and spoon measurements are metric. Conversion charts for cup and spoon measurements and oven temperatures appear on page 127.
A glossary explaining unfamiliar terms and ingredients appears on page 124.

STARTERS & SNACKS

We have lots of delicious entree ideas for beef, chicken, pork and veal, and lamb mince. All can be easily adapted to make lunches, snacks, light meals, even tasty party fare. You will find familiar favourites, like the Aussie meat pie and Scotch eggs, and some new recipes — olive mince bread, spicy nachos pie, and beef and ginger wontons, for instance — which have been inspired by international cuisines.

CHICKEN SOUP WITH PRAWN AND PORK WONTONS

½ cup (15g) dried Chinese
  mushrooms
100g uncooked prawns, shelled,
  finely chopped
100g minced pork and veal
1 green shallot, finely chopped
1 teaspoon dry sherry
1 teaspoon dark soy sauce
1 teaspoon brown sugar
¼ teaspoon sesame oil
200g packet gow gees pastry
1 (about 120g) carrot
1 stick celery
2 litres (8 cups) chicken stock
3 green shallots, sliced, extra

CHICKEN STOCK
1.5kg boiling chicken
2 medium leeks, sliced
2 (about 240g) carrots, chopped
1 bay leaf
1 teaspoon black peppercorns
2½ litres (10 cups) water

Place mushrooms in bowl, cover with boiling water, stand 20 minutes. Drain mushrooms, discard stems, finely chop caps.

Combine mushrooms, prawns, mince, shallot, sherry, sauce, sugar and oil in bowl; mix well. Place level teaspoons of mince mixture in centre of each wrapper, lightly brush edges of wrappers with water. Gather sides of wrappers around filling, pleating edges together to seal.

Add wontons to large pan of boiling water, boil, 3 minutes or until tender; drain.

Cut carrot and celery into thin strips. Bring chicken stock to boil, add carrot, celery, extra shallots and wontons, simmer until heated through.

Chicken Stock: Combine all ingredients in pan; bring to boil, simmer, covered, 3 hours. Strain stock into bowl; reserve chicken for another use. Cool stock, cover, refrigerate several hours or overnight. Skim fat from stock.

Serves 6.

■ Wontons can be made a day ahead; keep covered, in refrigerator.
■ Soup best made just before serving.
■ Freeze: Stock suitable.
■ Microwave: Suitable.

Wooden mat and china from Butler & Co.; bamboo steamer from The Culinary Delight.

paprika and mince, stir over heat until mince is browned. Add tomatoes, chilli powder and sugar, simmer, uncovered, until liquid is evaporated. Remove from heat, stir in rice; cool.

Add lettuce to large pan of boiling water, cook 30 seconds; drain, rinse under cold water; drain on absorbent paper. Divide mince mixture evenly between lettuce leaves, roll up firmly. Serve lettuce parcels with tarragon vinaigrette.

Tarragon Vinaigrette: Combine all ingredients in jar; shake well.

Serves 6 to 8.

- Recipe can be made 3 hours ahead.
- Storage: Covered, in refrigerator.
- Freeze: Not suitable.
- Microwave: Not suitable.

CROSTINI WITH OLIVE AND PIMIENTO TOPPING

8 slices Vienna loaf (about 2cm thick)
½ cup olive oil
2 cloves garlic, crushed
1½ cups (150g) grated mozzarella cheese

OLIVE AND PIMIENTO TOPPING
1 tablespoon olive oil
1 onion, chopped
1 clove garlic, crushed
750g minced beef
410g can tomatoes
¼ cup dry red wine
1 teaspoon sugar
1 tablespoon tomato paste
390g can pimientos, drained, sliced
½ cup black olives, halved

Lightly brush bread on both sides with combined oil and garlic; place in single layer on oven tray. Bake in moderately hot oven about 15 minutes or until lightly browned and crisp, turn halfway through cooking. Sprinkle bread evenly with cheese; grill until melted. Top with olive and pimiento topping.

Olive and Pimiento Topping: Heat oil in pan, add onion and garlic, cook, stirring, until onion is soft. Add mince, stir over heat until mince is browned. Stir in undrained crushed tomatoes, wine, sugar and paste. Bring to boil, simmer, uncovered, until mixture is thick. Stir in pimientos and olives, stir until hot.

Serves 8.

- Recipe best made just before serving.
- Freeze: Not suitable.
- Microwave: Not suitable.

LETTUCE PARCELS WITH TARRAGON VINAIGRETTE

⅓ cup long grain rice
2 tablespoons olive oil
1 onion, chopped
2 cloves garlic, crushed
2 teaspoons paprika
300g minced beef
2 (about 250g) tomatoes, peeled, chopped
pinch chilli powder
1 teaspoon sugar
12 cos lettuce leaves

TARRAGON VINAIGRETTE
2 tablespoons tarragon vinegar
¾ cup olive oil
½ teaspoon cracked black peppercorns
½ teaspoon sugar
1 teaspoon seeded mustard
1 clove garlic, crushed
1 small onion, finely chopped

Add rice to large pan of boiling water, boil, uncovered, until just tender; drain.

Heat oil in pan, add onion and garlic, cook, stirring, until onion is soft. Add

ABOVE LEFT: From left: Lettuce Parcels with Tarragon Vinaigrette, Crostini with Olive and Pimiento Topping.

TWO-MINCE SCONE CAKE WITH ROASTED PEPPERS

30g butter
1 onion, chopped
1 clove garlic, crushed
200g sausage mince
200g minced beef
1 egg, lightly beaten
2 tablespoons packaged breadcrumbs
1 teaspoon dried mixed herbs
310g can red kidney beans, rinsed, drained
¾ cup frozen peas, thawed
1 egg, lightly beaten, extra
1 tablespoon grated parmesan cheese

SCONE CAKE
2 cups self-raising flour
10g butter
2 tablespoons chopped fresh parsley
¼ cup grated tasty cheese
½ cup milk
½ cup water, approximately

ROASTED PEPPERS
3 large red peppers, sliced
2 tablespoons olive oil
2 teaspoons brown sugar
1 clove garlic, crushed

Lightly grease deep 20cm round cake pan, line base with paper; grease paper.

Heat butter in pan, add onion and garlic, cook, stirring, until onion is soft. Combine onion mixture, minces, egg, breadcrumbs, herbs, beans and peas in bowl; mix well.

Roll half of scone dough on lightly floured surface large enough to fit base of prepared pan, brush with a little extra egg. Press mince mixture firmly over dough, brush with a little more extra egg.

Roll remaining dough on floured surface large enough to cover mince mixture, place over mince, brush with remaining extra egg, sprinkle with cheese. Bake, uncovered, in moderate oven about 1¼ hours; cover cake if necessary. Serve scone cake with roasted peppers.

Scone Cake: Sift flour into bowl, rub in butter, stir in parsley and cheese. Stir in milk and enough water to mix to a soft dough. Knead on lightly floured surface until smooth.

Roasted Peppers: Combine peppers, oil, sugar and garlic in ovenproof dish; mix well. Bake, uncovered, in moderate oven about 50 minutes or until peppers are soft, stirring occasionally.

Serves 6.

◼ Recipe can be made 3 hours ahead.
◼ Storage: Covered, in refrigerator.
◼ Freeze: Cooked cake suitable.
◼ Microwave: Not suitable.

BELOW: Two-Mince Scone Cake with Roasted Peppers.

MUSHROOMS WITH PORK AND PINE NUT SEASONING

8 large flat mushrooms
2 tablespoons grated parmesan
   cheese
¼ teaspoon paprika

PORK AND PINE NUT SEASONING
1 tablespoon oil
1 small onion, chopped
125g minced pork and veal
2 tablespoons pine nuts
¼ cup stale breadcrumbs
1 egg white, lightly beaten
2 tablespoons chopped fresh basil
½ teaspoon cracked black
   peppercorns

Finely chop stalks of 4 mushrooms; discard remaining stalks. Place mushrooms on oven tray, top with pork and pine nut seasoning; sprinkle with cheese and paprika. Bake uncovered in moderate oven about 10 minutes or until tender.
Pork and Pine Nut Seasoning: Heat oil in pan, add onion, mince and nuts, stir over heat until mince is browned. Remove from heat, stir in reserved mushroom stalks, then remaining ingredients.

Serves 4.
- Seasoning can be made 3 hours ahead.
- Storage: Covered, in refrigerator.
- Freeze: Not suitable.
- Microwave: Not suitable.

MINCE AND BACON MEATBALLS WITH SAFFRON SAUCE

500g minced pork and veal
2 bacon rashers, chopped
1 cup (70g) stale breadcrumbs
2 cloves garlic, crushed
1 tablespoon chopped fresh
   coriander
1 egg
1 small chicken stock cube
1 tablespoon olive oil

SAFFRON SAUCE
1 tablespoon olive oil
2 cloves garlic, crushed
½ teaspoon paprika
pinch ground saffron
1 small chicken stock cube
½ cup water
2 tablespoons dry white wine
½ teaspoon sugar
1 teaspoon plain flour
2 teaspoons water, extra
⅓ cup sour cream

Process mince, bacon, breadcrumbs, garlic, coriander, egg and crumbled stock cube until finely minced. Roll 2 level teaspoons of mixture into balls.

Heat oil in pan, add meatballs, cook, shaking pan frequently, until well browned and tender; drain on absorbent paper. Serve with saffron sauce.
Saffron Sauce: Heat oil in pan, add garlic, paprika and saffron, cook, stirring, 1 minute. Stir in crumbled stock cube, water, wine, sugar and blended flour and extra water. Stir over heat until mixture boils and thickens slightly; remove from heat, stir in sour cream.

Serves 6.
- Recipe can be made a day ahead.
- Storage: Covered, in refrigerator.
- Freeze: Not suitable.
- Microwave: Not suitable.

CHEESY POTATO AND BEEF SLICE

1kg potatoes, chopped
30g butter
1 egg, lightly beaten
¼ cup packaged breadcrumbs
¼ cup grated tasty cheese
paprika

BEEF FILLING
1 tablespoon oil
500g minced beef
1 onion, chopped
410g can tomatoes
2 tablespoons tomato paste
1 tablespoon Worcestershire sauce
1 teaspoon beef stock powder
½ teaspoon dried basil leaves
1 tablespoon plain flour
⅓ cup water

Boil, steam or microwave potatoes until tender; drain. Mash potatoes in large bowl with butter, cool; stir in egg.

Sprinkle half the breadcrumbs over

base and sides of greased shallow ovenproof dish (4 cup capacity). Spread a third potato mixture over base of prepared dish, top with beef filling. Spoon remaining potato into piping bag, pipe over filling, sprinkle with remaining breadcrumbs, cheese and paprika. Bake, uncovered, in moderate oven about 35 minutes or until lightly browned.

Beef Filling: Heat oil in pan, add mince and onion, stir over heat until mince is browned. Stir in undrained crushed tomatoes, paste, sauce, stock powder and basil. Bring to boil, simmer, uncovered, until mince is tender. Stir in blended flour and water, stir over heat until mixture boils and thickens.

Serves 4.

- ■ Recipe can be made a day ahead.
- ■ Storage: Covered, in refrigerator.
- ■ Freeze: Suitable.
- ■ Microwave: Suitable.

PARSNIP CAKES WITH SPICED MINCE

1 tablespoon oil
1 onion, chopped
1 teaspoon turmeric
1 teaspoon garam masala
1 teaspoon ground coriander
½ teaspoon ground cumin
500g minced beef
425g can tomato puree
½ cup water
1 small beef stock cube
2 teaspoons sugar
1 tablespoon chopped fresh parsley

PARSNIP CAKES
3 medium (about 500g) parsnips, coarsely grated
2 tablespoons plain flour
2 eggs, lightly beaten
2 tablespoons oil

Heat oil in pan, add onion, turmeric, garam masala, coriander and cumin, cook, stirring, until onion is soft. Add mince, cook, stirring, until mince is well browned. Add puree, water, crumbled

stock cube and sugar, bring to boil, simmer, uncovered, until mince is tender. Spoon mince mixture over parsnip cakes, sprinkle with parsley.

Parsnip Cakes: Combine parsnips, flour and eggs in bowl; mix well. Heat oil in pan, drop ⅓ cups of mixture into pan, flatten with egg slide, cook on each side until crisp; drain on absorbent paper.

Serves 4.

- ■ Mince can be made a day ahead.
- ■ Storage: Covered, in refrigerator.
- ■ Freeze: Mince suitable.
- ■ Microwave: Not suitable.

LEFT: From left: Mince and Bacon Meatballs with Saffron Sauce, Mushrooms with Pork and Pine Nut Seasoning.
ABOVE: From top: Parsnip Cakes with Spiced Mince, Cheesy Potato and Beef Slice.

Left: Fabric from Lillywhites; Mexican glass plates from Butler & Co.

7

constantly over simmering water until just beginning to thicken, whisk in butter gradually, whisking constantly until thick and smooth.

Serves 6.

- Pithivier can be prepared a day ahead; sauce is best made just before serving.
- Storage: Covered, in refrigerator.
- Freeze: Uncooked pithivier suitable.
- Microwave: Not suitable.

LIVER AND MINCE TERRINE

1 bunch (40 leaves) English spinach
2 medium leeks
1 tablespoon oil
5 bacon rashers, chopped
500g minced pork and veal
150g chicken livers, chopped
¾ cup stale breadcrumbs
½ cup grated fresh parmesan cheese
½ cup grated tasty cheese
2 cloves garlic, crushed
2 teaspoons chopped fresh thyme
2 teaspoons chopped fresh sage
½ teaspoon cracked black
**   peppercorns**
1 tablespoon dry sherry

Place spinach in pan, cover, cook gently until wilted. Drain, rinse under cold water. Squeeze excess water from spinach; chop spinach roughly.

Wash leek, slice lengthways but only halfway through so that leek can be opened up like a book. Add 12 outer leaves of leek to pan of boiling water, boil 3 minutes, drain; rinse under cold water, drain well. Reserve remaining leek.

Lightly grease 11cm x 23cm loaf dish (6 cup capacity); line base and sides of dish with cooked leek leaves, allowing ends to overhang sides of dish.

Chop reserved leek. Heat oil in pan, add reserved leek, cook, stirring, until soft.

Combine leek mixture and spinach with remaining ingredients in bowl; mix well.

Spoon mixture into lined dish. Fold leek leaves over to cover mince mixture, press down firmly, cover dish with greased foil, place on oven tray. Bake in moderate oven about 1¾ hours or until firm; cool. Refrigerate terrine overnight.

Serves 6 to 8.

- Recipe best made a day ahead.
- Storage: Covered, in refrigerator.
- Freeze: Not suitable.
- Microwave: Spinach and leek suitable.

BEEF PITHIVIER WITH BEARNAISE SAUCE

2 sheets ready-rolled puff pastry
1 egg, lightly beaten

FILLING
1 tablespoon oil
1 onion, sliced
2 cloves garlic, crushed
500g minced beef
1½ cups (110g) stale breadcrumbs
3 bacon rashers, chopped
2 small beef stock cubes
1 egg, lightly beaten
¼ cup water

BEARNAISE SAUCE
⅓ cup white vinegar
6 black peppercorns
2 teaspoons dried tarragon leaves
1 bay leaf
2 egg yolks
200g butter, chopped

Cut a 24cm round from 1 sheet of pastry and a 23cm round from other sheet. Place smaller round onto lightly greased oven tray, top with filling, leaving a 1cm border. Brush border with a little egg, top with larger round of pastry, press edges together with fork. Using sharp knife, mark pastry with swirl design from centre to side; do not cut all the way through pastry. Brush pastry lightly with remaining egg. Bake in moderately hot oven about 30 minutes or until browned and puffed. Serve with bearnaise sauce.

Filling: Heat oil in pan, add onion and garlic, cook, stirring, until onion is soft. Combine onion mixture, mince, breadcrumbs, bacon, crumbled stock cubes, egg and water in bowl; mix well.

Bearnaise Sauce: Combine vinegar, peppercorns and herbs in pan, bring to boil; simmer, uncovered, until reduced to 1 tablespoon; strain, reserve liquid. Combine egg yolks and vinegar mixture in bowl or in top half of double saucepan, place over pan of simmering water. Whisk

ABOVE LEFT: Beef Pithivier with Bearnaise Sauce.
RIGHT: Clockwise from left: Chilli Eggs with Crispy Coconut Crust, Liver and Mince Terrine, Oriental Lettuce Cups.

Above left: Linen from Archway Tablewares.
Right: Wooden mat and plates from Butler & Co.

ORIENTAL LETTUCE CUPS

300g minced pork and veal
2 cloves garlic, crushed
2 green shallots, chopped
1 (about 120g) carrot, coarsely grated
230g can sliced water chestnuts, drained
1 small red pepper, thinly sliced
1 tablespoon oyster sauce
2 teaspoons hoi sin sauce
1 tablespoon light soy sauce
½ teaspoon sesame oil
1 tablespoon oil
6 lettuce leaves

Combine mince, garlic, shallots, carrot, chestnuts, pepper, sauces and sesame oil in bowl; cover, refrigerate 1 hour.

Heat oil in pan or wok, add mince mixture, stir-fry until mince is browned; cool. Spoon mixture onto lettuce leaves just before serving.

Serves 6.

- Recipe can be made 4 hours ahead.
- Storage: Covered, in refrigerator.
- Freeze: Not suitable.
- Microwave: Not suitable.

CHILLI EGGS WITH CRISPY COCONUT CRUST

6 hard-boiled eggs
250g minced pork and veal
1 clove garlic, crushed
¼ teaspoon dried chilli flakes
1 tablespoon chopped fresh coriander
plain flour
2 eggs, lightly beaten
2 cups (140g) shredded coconut
oil for deep-frying

SAUCE
½ cup water
½ cup sugar
1 tablespoon white vinegar
1 teaspoon light soy sauce

Cut hard-boiled eggs in half lengthways, remove yolks. Mash yolks in bowl with fork, add mince, garlic, chilli and coriander; mix well. Divide mince mixture into 12 portions, shape portions over egg white halves to form egg shapes; cover, refrigerate 1 hour.

Just before serving, toss egg halves in flour, shake away excess flour, dip into beaten eggs, toss in coconut. Deep-fry eggs in hot oil in batches, until browned; drain on absorbent paper. Serve eggs hot with sauce.

Sauce: Combine all ingredients in pan, stir over heat without boiling, until sugar is dissolved. Bring to boil, simmer, uncovered, about 5 minutes or until sauce is slightly syrupy.

Makes 12.

- Recipe can be prepared a day ahead.
- Storage: Covered, in refrigerator.
- Freeze: Not suitable.
- Microwave: Not suitable.

DONOR KEBAB ROLLS

²⁄₃ cup hummus
4 Lebanese bread rounds
6 lettuce leaves, shredded
1 red Spanish onion, sliced
1 large (about 250g) tomato, sliced
2 tablespoons barbecue sauce
2 tablespoons chopped fresh parsley

PATTIES
400g minced beef
²⁄₃ cup stale breadcrumbs
2 tablespoons tomato sauce
2 tablespoons chopped fresh parsley
½ teaspoon ground cumin
½ teaspoon ground cardamom
2 tablespoons oil

Spread quarter of the hummus over each bread round. Top with quarter of the lettuce, onion rings and tomato, then 3 patties, some sauce and parsley. Roll bread up firmly, roll in greaseproof paper.
Patties: Combine mince, bread crumbs, sauce, parsley, cumin and cardamom in bowl, mix well. Shape mixture into 12 patties. Heat oil in pan, add patties, cook until browned and cooked through; drain on absorbent paper.

Serves 4.
- Recipe best assembled close to serving; patties can be made a day ahead.
- Freeze: Patties suitable.
- Microwave: Not suitable.

CRUNCHY MEATBALLS WITH TABBOULEH

350g minced beef
2 tablespoons chopped fresh mint
2 tablespoons chopped fresh parsley
2 cloves garlic, crushed
2 eggs, lightly beaten
1 cup (160g) cracked wheat
oil for deep-frying

TABBOULEH
2 cups chopped fresh parsley
¾ cup chopped fresh mint
1 onion, finely chopped
2 large (about 500g) tomatoes, finely chopped
1 red pepper, finely chopped
1 tablespoon olive oil

GARLIC DRESSING
¾ cup plain yogurt
1½ tablespoons lemon juice
4 cloves garlic, crushed
1 tablespoon chopped fresh chives

Combine mince, mint, parsley and garlic in bowl; mix well. Shape level tablespoons of mixture into balls, dip into eggs, roll in cracked wheat.
Just before serving, deep-fry meatballs in hot oil until lightly browned and cooked through; drain on absorbent paper. Serve with tabbouleh and garlic dressing.

Tabbouleh: Combine all ingredients in bowl; mix well.
Garlic Dressing: Combine all ingredients in bowl; mix well.

Serves 6.
- Recipe can be prepared 6 hours ahead.
- Storage: Covered, in refrigerator.
- Freeze: Not suitable.
- Microwave: Not suitable.

SPICY NACHOS PIE

200g packet cheese flavoured corn chips
½ cup stale breadcrumbs
²⁄₃ cup finely grated tasty cheese
2 eggs, lightly beaten
300g carton sour cream
½ cup grated tasty cheese, extra
¼ teaspoon paprika
pinch chilli powder

FILLING
1 tablespoon oil
1 onion, chopped
2 cloves garlic, crushed
500g minced beef
1 green pepper, chopped
1 teaspoon ground cumin
¼ teaspoon chilli powder
410g can tomatoes
1 teaspoon beef stock powder
2 tablespoons tomato paste
310g can red kidney beans, rinsed, drained

Process corn chips until finely crushed. Combine crushed chips with breadcrumbs, cheese and eggs. Press mixture evenly over base and side of greased 23cm pie plate. Bake in moderately hot oven about 10 minutes or until lightly browned; cool.
Spoon filling into pastry case, spread sour cream over filling, top with extra cheese, sprinkle with paprika and chilli. Bake in moderate oven about 15 minutes or until top is set.
Filling: Heat oil in pan, add onion and garlic, cook, stirring, until onion is soft. Add mince, pepper, cumin and chilli, stir over heat until mince is browned. Add undrained crushed tomatoes and remaining ingredients, bring to boil, simmer, uncovered, until mixture is thick.

Serves 6.
- Recipe best made on day of serving.
- Storage: Covered, in refrigerator.
- Freeze: Not suitable.
- Microwave: Not suitable.

LEFT: From top: Donor Kebab Rolls, Crunchy Meatballs with Tabbouleh, Spicy Nachos Pie.

China from Archway Tablewares.

SPICY RISSOLES WITH NUTTY SAUCE

400g minced beef
1 egg
¾ cup stale breadcrumbs
2 teaspoons sambal oelek
2 cloves garlic, crushed
1 teaspoon fish sauce
2 tablespoons chopped fresh
  coriander
½ teaspoon grated lime rind
oil for shallow-frying

NUTTY SAUCE
½ cup white vinegar
⅓ cup castor sugar
1 tablespoon finely chopped unsalted
  roasted peanuts
½ teaspoon sambal oelek
2 teaspoons chopped fresh coriander

Combine mince, egg, breadcrumbs, sambal oelek, garlic, sauce, coriander and rind in bowl; mix well. Roll level tablespoons of mixture into balls. Shallow-fry rissoles in hot oil until cooked through; drain on absorbent paper. Serve rissoles with nutty sauce.
Nutty Sauce: Combine vinegar and sugar in small pan; stir over heat, without boiling, until sugar is dissolved. Bring to boil, simmer, uncovered, 8 minutes or until mixture is thick and syrupy. Remove from heat, stir in peanuts and sambal oelek; cool. Stir in coriander just before serving.

Makes about 20.

- ■ Rissoles and sauce can be made a day ahead.
- ■ Storage: Covered, in refrigerator.
- ■ Freeze: Meatballs suitable.
- ■ Microwave: Not suitable.

SAVOURY MINCE WITH THREE PEPPERS

1 tablespoon oil
1 onion, sliced
1 clove garlic, crushed
½ teaspoon grated fresh ginger
500g minced beef
1 (about 150g) apple, chopped
1 small green pepper, chopped
1 small red pepper, chopped
1 small yellow pepper, chopped
3 sticks celery, chopped
1 large beef stock cube
1½ cups water
2 tablespoons dark soy sauce
2 tablespoons tomato sauce
2 tablespoons sweet chilli sauce
1 tablespoon cornflour
2 tablespoons water, extra
2 tablespoons lemon juice
1 tablespoon pine nuts
2 green shallots, chopped

Heat oil in pan, add onion, garlic and ginger, cook, stirring, until onion is soft. Add mince, stir over heat until browned. Stir in apple, peppers, celery, crumbled stock cube, water and sauces. Bring to boil, simmer, covered, 10 minutes. Stir in blended cornflour and extra water with lemon juice. Stir over heat until mixture boils and thickens. Serve, sprinkled with nuts and shallots. Serve with steamed or boiled rice, if desired.

Serves 4 to 6.

- ■ Recipe can be made a day ahead.
- ■ Storage: Covered, in refrigerator.
- ■ Freeze: Not suitable.
- ■ Microwave: Not suitable.

ABOVE: From top: Spicy Rissoles with Nutty Sauce, Savoury Mince with Three Peppers.

China from Amy's Tableware.

ANGEL PASTA SOUP WITH MEATBALLS AND SAGE

1 litre (4 cups) water
2 teaspoons beef stock powder
2 (about 240g) carrots, thinly sliced
125g angel hair pasta

MEATBALLS
350g minced pork and veal
1 egg
1 egg white
1½ tablespoons chopped fresh sage
2 tablespoons grated parmesan cheese
½ cup stale breadcrumbs
1 (about 130g) tomato, peeled, chopped
1 large onion, finely chopped
5 cloves garlic, crushed
¼ teaspoon cracked black peppercorns
2 tablespoons oil

Heat water and stock powder in pan, add carrots, bring to boil, simmer, covered, about 10 minutes or until carrots are tender. Add meatballs and pasta, simmer 5 minutes or until meatballs are heated through and pasta is just tender.

Meatballs: Process mince, egg, egg white, sage, cheese, breadcrumbs, tomato, onion, garlic and peppercorns until well combined. Transfer mixture to bowl, cover, refrigerate 30 minutes.

Roll level tablespoons of mixture into balls. Heat oil in pan, add meatballs, cook, shaking pan frequently, until well browned; drain on absorbent paper.

Serves 4.

- Meatballs can be made a day ahead.
- Storage: Covered, in refrigerator.
- Freeze: Meatballs suitable.
- Microwave: Soup suitable.

PORK AND VEAL PATE WITH LEEK MARMALADE

1 large leek
4 bacon rashers
3 teaspoons canned drained green peppercorns
150g chicken livers
300g minced pork and veal
1 small onion, chopped
125g frozen spinach, thawed, drained
½ teaspoon dried oregano leaves
½ teaspoon dried marjoram leaves
1 egg, lightly beaten
1 tablespoon plain flour
2 teaspoons juniper berries

LEEK MARMALADE
1 tablespoon olive oil
½ cup water
¼ cup sugar
2 tablespoons marmalade

Cut 6cm piece from white part of leek, reserve remaining leek for marmalade. Add leek to pan of boiling water, boil until just tender, drain; rinse under cold water, drain well. Cut leek into 12 thin slices.

Lightly grease 4 ovenproof moulds (1 cup capacity). Place 3 slices of leek into each mould, line moulds with bacon; sprinkle in peppercorns to fill gaps between leek slices.

Process livers, mince, onion, spinach and herbs until well combined. Transfer mixture to bowl, stir in egg, flour and berries; mix well. Press mixture evenly into prepared moulds; cover with foil. Stand moulds in baking dish, pour in enough boiling water to come halfway up sides of moulds; bake in moderate oven about 40 minutes or until cooked through; cool.

Refrigerate moulds 3 hours or overnight. Serve pate with leek marmalade.
Leek Marmalade: Chop reserved leek. Heat oil in pan, add leek, cook, stirring, until soft, add water and sugar. Bring mixture to boil, simmer, covered, 10 minutes.

Simmer, uncovered, further 5 minutes; stir in marmalade. Blend or process leek mixture until smooth, cool.

Serves 4.

- Recipe can be made 2 days ahead.
- Storage: Covered, in refrigerator.
- Freeze: Not suitable.
- Microwave: Marmalade suitable.

BELOW: From top: Angel Pasta Soup with Meatballs and Sage, Pork and Veal Pate with Leek Marmalade.

Plate, bowl, copper saucepan, placemats and cloth from Lillywhites.

balls, cook until heated through. Serve sprinkled with cheese.

Meatballs: Combine mince, breadcrumbs, herbs, egg yolk and cheese in bowl; mix well. Roll 2 level teaspoons of mixture into balls. Shallow-fry meatballs in hot oil until browned and cooked through.

Serves 4 to 6.

- Soup and meatballs can be made separately a day ahead.
- Storage: Covered, in refrigerator.
- Freeze: Meatballs suitable.
- Microwave: Soup suitable.

EGGPLANT SLICES WITH TOMATO MINCE TOPPING

2 (about 600g) eggplants
coarse cooking salt
⅔ cup olive oil
1 tablespoon chopped fresh basil

TOMATO MINCE TOPPING
1 tablespoon olive oil
1 onion, finely chopped
2 cloves garlic, crushed
1 small green pepper, chopped
250g minced beef
410g can tomatoes
½ teaspoon ground cinnamon
1 tablespoon sweet chilli sauce
1 tablespoon dark soy sauce
1 tablespoon chopped fresh basil
1 tablespoon chopped fresh parsley

Cut eggplants into 1½cm thick slices, sprinkle with salt; stand 30 minutes. Rinse eggplant slices under cold water, pat dry with absorbent paper.

Heat oil in pan, add eggplant, cook in batches until browned on both sides; drain on absorbent paper. Spoon tomato mince topping onto eggplant slices, sprinkle with basil.

Tomato Mince Topping: Heat oil in pan, add onion and garlic, cook, stirring until onion is soft. Add pepper and mince, stir over heat until mince is well browned. Add remaining ingredients, bring to boil, simmer, uncovered, until liquid is evaporated and mixture is thick.

Serves 4 to 6.

- Topping can be made a day ahead.
- Storage: Covered, in refrigerator.
- Freeze: Topping suitable.
- Microwave: Not suitable.

PASTA WITH MUSHROOMS AND BASIL

1 tablespoon oil
1 onion, sliced
3 cloves garlic, crushed
500g minced beef
250g baby mushrooms, sliced
½ cup dry white wine
2 x 410g cans tomatoes
1 small beef stock cube
¼ cup shredded fresh basil
2 tablespoons chopped fresh chives
250g spiral pasta

Heat oil in pan, add onion and garlic, cook, stirring, until onion is soft. Add mince, stir over heat until well browned. Add mushrooms, cook until tender. Stir in wine, undrained crushed tomatoes and crumbled stock cube. Bring to boil, simmer, uncovered, about 15 minutes or until sauce is slightly thickened; stir in herbs.

Meanwhile, add pasta to large pan of boiling water, boil, uncovered, until just tender; drain. Stir sauce through pasta.

Serves 4.

- Recipe can be made a day ahead.
- Storage: Covered, in refrigerator.
- Freeze: Suitable.
- Microwave: Suitable.

SPINACH AND MEATBALL SOUP

1 tablespoon oil
1 onion, chopped
1 clove garlic, crushed
1 large (about 200g) potato, chopped
1 litre (4 cups) water
2 small chicken stock cubes
1 bunch (40 leaves) English spinach, chopped
½ cup cream
grated fresh parmesan cheese

MEATBALLS
250g minced beef
½ cup stale breadcrumbs
2 tablespoons chopped fresh basil
1 tablespoon chopped fresh chives
1 egg yolk
½ cup grated fresh parmesan cheese
oil for shallow-frying

Heat oil in pan, add onion and garlic, cook, stirring, until onion is soft. Add potato, cook, stirring, further 5 minutes. Stir in water and crumbled stock cubes. Bring to boil, simmer, covered, about 10 minutes or until potato is tender. Stir in spinach, simmer, uncovered, further 5 minutes; stir in cream.

Blend or process soup in batches until smooth. Return soup to pan with meat-

ABOVE LEFT: Pasta with Mushrooms and Basil.
RIGHT: Clockwise from left: Beef and Pepper Tacos with Spicy Cream, Spinach and Meatball Soup, Eggplant Slices with Tomato Mince Topping.

Right: Pots and plates from Something Special Gallery.

BEEF AND PEPPER TACOS WITH SPICY CREAM

1 tablespoon olive oil
2 onions, sliced
1 tablespoon white vinegar
1 red pepper
1 green pepper
1 tablespoon olive oil, extra
1 onion, chopped, extra
2 cloves garlic, crushed
500g minced beef
1 teaspoon ground cumin
1/4 teaspoon chilli powder
2 tablespoons tomato paste
1 small beef stock cube
1/4 cup water
8 taco shells

SPICY CREAM
1 teaspoon ground cumin
1/2 teaspoon ground coriander
1/4 teaspoon chilli powder
2/3 cup sour cream

Heat oil in pan, add onions, cook, stirring, until soft; add vinegar, cook 1 minute. Quarter peppers, remove seeds and membrane. Grill peppers, skin side up, until skin blisters and blackens. Peel away skin, cut peppers into thin strips.

Heat extra oil in pan, add extra onion and garlic, cook, stirring, until onion is soft. Add mince, cook, stirring, until mince is browned. Add cumin and chilli, cook, stirring, 1 minute. Add tomato paste, crumbled stock cube and water; bring to boil, simmer, uncovered, until mixture is thickened slightly.

Heat taco shells according to directions on packet just before serving. Fill taco shells with mince mixture, top with onions and peppers, then spicy cream.

Spicy Cream: Heat cumin, coriander and chilli in dry pan until fragrant; cool. Combine spices and sour cream in small bowl; mix well.

Makes 8.

- Recipe can be prepared a day ahead.
- Storage: Covered, in refrigerator.
- Freeze: Not suitable.
- Microwave: Not suitable.

BEEF AND CHICK PEA SOUP

1 tablespoon oil
1 onion, chopped
2 cloves garlic, crushed
400g minced beef
1 red pepper, chopped
410g can tomatoes
2 tablespoons tomato paste
310g can chick peas, rinsed, drained
310g can red kidney beans, rinsed,
    drained
2 cups water
2 small beef stock cubes
¼ teaspoon chilli powder
1 teaspoon dried mixed herbs
½ teaspoon sugar
½ cup water, approximately, extra

Heat oil in large pan, add onion and garlic, cook, stirring, until onion is soft. Add mince, stir over heat until browned, add pepper, undrained crushed tomatoes, paste, chick peas, beans, water, crumbled stock cubes, chilli powder, herbs and sugar. Bring to boil, simmer, covered, 30 minutes. Blend or process mixture until well combined. Return soup to pan, stir in enough extra water to make soup as thin as desired. Stir over heat until heated through.

Serves 4.

- Recipe can be made 2 days ahead.
- Storage: Covered, in refrigerator.
- Freeze: Suitable.
- Microwave: Suitable.

MUSHROOM AND BEEF FLANS

2 cups plain flour
150g butter
1 egg yolk
1 teaspoon lemon juice
1 tablespoon water, approximately
2 eggs, lightly beaten
⅔ cup thickened cream
2 tablespoons milk

FILLING
1 tablespoon oil
1 onion, chopped
1 clove garlic, crushed
150g minced beef
100g mushrooms, chopped
1 teaspoon chopped fresh basil
¼ teaspoon dried oregano leaves
2 (about 250g) tomatoes, peeled,
    chopped

Sift flour into large bowl, rub in butter, stir in yolk, juice and enough water to make ingredients cling together. Press dough into ball, knead on floured surface until smooth, cover; refrigerate 30 minutes.

Divide pastry into 8 portions. Roll each portion on lightly floured surface large enough to line 8 greased 10cm flan tins. Ease pastry into tins, trim edges. Place tins on oven trays, line pastry with paper, fill with dried beans or rice. Bake in moderately hot oven 7 minutes, remove paper and beans, bake further 7 minutes or until pastry is lightly browned.

Divide filling between pastry cases, pour over combined eggs, cream and milk. Bake flans in moderate oven about 30 minutes or until browned.

Filling: Heat oil in pan, add onion and garlic, cook, stirring, until onion is soft, add mince and mushrooms, stir over heat until mince is well browned. Stir in herbs and tomatoes, simmer, uncovered, until liquid is evaporated.

Makes 8.

- Recipe can be made a day ahead.
- Storage: Covered, in refrigerator.
- Freeze: Suitable.
- Microwave: Not suitable.

AUSSIE MEAT PIES

2 cups plain flour
125g lard, chopped
2 eggs, lightly beaten
2 tablespoons water, approximately
2 sheets ready-rolled puff pastry
1 egg yolk, lightly beaten

FILLING
30g lard
2 onions, chopped
900g minced beef
1/4 cup Worcestershire sauce
1/4 cup dark soy sauce
2 teaspoons beef stock powder
2 cups water
1/2 teaspoon ground allspice
2 tablespoons cornflour
2 tablespoons water, extra

Sift flour into bowl, rub in lard. Add eggs and enough water to make ingredients cling together. Press dough into ball, knead gently on floured surface until smooth, cover, refrigerate 30 minutes.

Divide dough into 8 portions. Roll each portion on lightly floured surface large enough to line 11cm pie tins. Trim away excess pastry. Place tins on oven tray, line pastry with paper, fill with dried beans or rice. Bake in moderately hot oven about 8 minutes, remove paper and beans, bake further 8 minutes or until pastry is lightly browned; cool.

Spoon cold filling into pastry cases. Cut 8 x 12cm rounds from puff pastry, brush edges of pastry base with a little egg yolk, gently press puff pastry tops into place; trim edges. Brush tops with a little more egg yolk. Make 2 small slits in centre of pies, place on oven trays, bake in moderately hot oven about 15 minutes or until lightly browned. Serve hot with tomato sauce.

Filling: Heat lard in pan, add onion, cook, stirring, until soft. Add mince, stir over heat until browned. Stir in sauces, stock powder, water and allspice. Bring to boil, simmer, covered, 20 minutes. Stir in blended cornflour and extra water, stir over heat until mixture boils and thickens.

Makes 8.

- Recipe can be made a day ahead.
- Storage: Covered, in refrigerator.
- Freeze: Suitable.
- Microwave: Not suitable.

FAR LEFT: From left: Beef and Chick Pea Soup, Mushroom and Beef Flans.
LEFT: Aussie Meat Pies.

Far left: China and serviette from Archway Tablewares.

PORK SPIRALS

7 dried Chinese mushrooms
1 tablespoon oil
¼ teaspoon sesame oil
300g minced pork and veal
1 teaspoon grated fresh ginger
1 tablespoon oyster sauce
¼ cup drained chopped water
  chestnuts
2 green shallots, chopped
1 teaspoon cornflour
¼ cup water
oil for shallow-frying

PASTRY
2 cups plain flour
¾ cup boiling water, approximately

Place mushrooms in bowl, cover with hot water, stand 20 minutes. Drain mushrooms, discard stalks, chop caps finely.

Heat oils in pan, add mince and ginger, cook, stirring, until mince is well browned. Add mushrooms, sauce, water chestnuts, shallots and blended cornflour and water, stir over heat until mixture boils and thickens, remove from heat; cool.

Divide pastry into 16 portions. Roll each portion into a 5cm x 20cm rectangle. Spoon a level tablespoon of mince mixture along centre of rectangle, brush edges with water. Roll up pastry from long side to enclose filling; roll into a spiral, secure end with water. Repeat with remaining pastry and filling. Cook spirals in hot oil on both sides, in batches, until browned; drain on absorbent paper.
Pastry: Sift flour into bowl, stir in enough water to mix to a firm dough. Knead dough on lightly floured surface until smooth, cover, stand 30 minutes.

Makes 16.

■ Mince can be made a day ahead.
■ Storage: Covered, in refrigerator.
■ Freeze: Not suitable.
■ Microwave: Filling suitable.

CHEESY RICE CROQUETTES

2 tablespoons olive oil
1 onion, chopped
1 clove garlic, crushed
300g minced pork and veal
400g can tomatoes
½ cup short grain rice
2 small chicken stock cubes
1½ cups water
2 tablespoons tomato paste
1 tablespoon chopped fresh basil
3 cups (210g) stale breadcrumbs
100g mozzarella cheese
plain flour
2 eggs, lightly beaten
2 tablespoons milk
1¼ cups (125g) packaged
  breadcrumbs
oil for deep-frying

Heat olive oil in pan, add onion and garlic, cook, stirring, until onion is soft. Add mince, cook, stirring, until well browned. Stir in undrained crushed tomatoes, rice,

crumbled stock cubes, water, paste and basil. Bring to boil, simmer, uncovered, about 12 minutes or until rice is tender and mixture is thick; cool. Stir in stale breadcrumbs; refrigerate until cold.

Cut cheese into 1cm x 5cm pieces. Roll 2 tablespoons of mince mixture into log, press 1 piece of cheese in centre, roll into croquette shape to enclose cheese. Repeat using remaining mince mixture and cheese.

Toss croquettes in flour, shake away excess flour. Dip into combined eggs and milk, toss in packaged breadcrumbs.

Just before serving, deep-fry croquettes in hot oil until browned. Drain on absorbent paper.

Serves 6 to 8.

■ Recipe can be prepared a day ahead.
■ Storage: Covered, in refrigerator.
■ Freeze: Suitable.
■ Microwave: Not suitable.

SPICY SAUSAGE PAN PIZZA

1 small (about 250g) eggplant, sliced
coarse cooking salt
2 tablespoons olive oil
150g mushrooms, chopped
1 tablespoon tomato paste
¾ cup ricotta cheese
1 (about 130g) tomato, seeded,
**   chopped**
1 red Spanish onion, finely chopped

PIZZA DOUGH
7g sachet granulated yeast
1 teaspoon sugar
1 cup warm milk
2 cups plain flour
¼ cup grated fresh parmesan cheese
¼ cup sesame seeds, toasted

SPICY SAUSAGES
125g minced beef
1 egg
1 teaspoon beef stock powder
1 clove garlic, crushed
¼ teaspoon dried thyme leaves
¼ teaspoon dried rosemary leaves
1 tablespoon chopped fresh parsley
2 teaspoons cracked black
**   peppercorns**
1½ cups (110g) stale breadcrumbs
1 tablespoon olive oil

Sprinkle eggplant with salt, stand 30 minutes. Rinse eggplant under cold water, pat dry with absorbent paper.

Brush eggplant with half the oil, add to hot pan, cook in batches until browned on both sides; drain on absorbent paper. Heat remaining oil in pan, add mushrooms, cook, stirring, until soft.

Roll pizza dough on lightly floured surface large enough to line base of greased 23cm springform tin. Lift dough into tin, spread with combined paste and cheese, top with sliced sausages, eggplant, mushroom mixture, and combined tomato and onion. Place tin on oven tray, bake in moderately hot oven 20 minutes, cover,

reduce heat to moderate, bake further 45 minutes or until cooked through.
Pizza Dough: Combine yeast, sugar and milk in bowl; cover, stand in warm place about 10 minutes or until mixture is frothy.

Sift flour into large bowl, stir in cheese and seeds. Stir in yeast mixture, mix to a soft sticky dough, cover, stand in warm place about 45 minutes or until dough is doubled in size. Knead dough on lightly floured surface about 5 minutes or until smooth and elastic.
Spicy Sausages: Process mince, egg, stock powder, garlic, herbs, peppercorns and breadcrumbs until combined. Divide mixture in half, roll each portion into a sausage about 2cm thick. Heat oil in pan, add sausages, cook until cooked through; drain on absorbent paper.

Serves 6 to 8.

■ Sausages can be made a day ahead. Recipe can be prepared 4 hours ahead.
■ Storage: Covered, in refrigerator.
■ Freeze: Uncooked dough and spicy sausages suitable.
■ Microwave: Not suitable.

LEFT: From left: Pork Spirals, Cheesy Rice Croquettes.
ABOVE: Spicy Sausage Pan Pizza.

Left: Tray and napkins from Lillywhites. Above: Jug from Archway Tablewares.

PIROSHKI

1½ cups self-raising flour
30g butter
2 teaspoons cracked black
    peppercorns
½ cup milk, approximately

FILLING
1 tablespoon oil
1 onion, chopped
2 cloves garlic, crushed
250g minced beef
400g can tomatoes
1 cup (80g) finely shredded cabbage
1 tablespoon light soy sauce

Sift flour into bowl, rub in butter, stir in peppercorns and enough milk to form a soft dough. Knead dough gently on lightly floured surface until smooth. Divide dough into 4 portions, roll each portion on lightly floured surface to an 18cm round. Place quarter of the filling in centre of each round; brush edges with a little milk, fold in half to enclose filling. Pinch edges

together. Place on lightly greased oven trays, brush with a little more milk, bake in moderately hot oven about 15 minutes or until lightly browned.

Filling: Heat oil in pan, add onion and garlic, cook, stirring, until onion is soft. Add mince, stir over heat until mince is well browned. Stir in undrained crushed tomatoes, cabbage and sauce. Bring to boil, simmer, uncovered, about 10 minutes or until liquid is evaporated and mixture is thick; cool.

Makes 4.

- Piroshki can be made a day ahead.
- Storage: Covered, in refrigerator.
- Freeze: Suitable.
- Microwave: Not suitable.

BURGHUL AND POTATO TOPPED BAKE

¼ cup oil
1 onion, chopped
750g minced beef
1 small beef stock cube
½ teaspoon celery salt
2 tablespoons sultanas
2 tablespoons pine nuts, toasted
1 teaspoon ground cinnamon
1½ tablespoons cornflour
1 cup water
2 tablespoons chopped fresh parsley

BURGHUL POTATO TOPPING
½ cup burghul
3 (about 600g) potatoes
30g butter
1 egg, lightly beaten
¼ teaspoon ground allspice
¼ cup chopped fresh parsley

Heat oil in pan, add onion, cook, stirring, until soft. Add mince, stir over heat until browned, stir in crumbled stock cube, salt, sultanas, pine nuts, cinnamon and blended cornflour and water. Stir over heat until mixture boils and thickens.

Spread mixture into ovenproof dish (6 cup capacity), spread with topping. Bake, uncovered, in moderate oven about 35 minutes or until topping is lightly browned. Serve sprinkled with parsley.

Burghul Potato Topping: Place burghul in bowl, cover with water, stand 1 hour. Drain burghul, squeeze excess moisture from burghul. Boil, steam or microwave potatoes until tender. Drain potatoes, mash with butter until smooth. Combine burghul, potato, egg, allspice and parsley in bowl; mix well.

Serves 4.

- Recipe can be made a day ahead.
- Storage: Covered, in refrigerator.
- Freeze: Suitable.
- Microwave: Suitable.

CRISPY PANCAKES WITH WATER CHESTNUT FILLING

2 eggs, lightly beaten
2 tablespoons milk
plain flour
¾ cup packaged breadcrumbs
⅓ cup sesame seeds
oil for shallow-frying

FILLING
1 tablespoon oil
¼ teaspoon sesame oil
4 green shallots, chopped
1 teaspoon ground cumin
2 whole star anise
500g minced beef
2 teaspoons cornflour
¼ cup water
½ teaspoon sugar
2 tablespoons hoi sin sauce
230g can water chestnuts, drained, chopped

PANCAKES
¾ cup plain flour
3 eggs, lightly beaten
1 tablespoon oil
1 cup milk

Spread filling evenly over pancakes, leaving a 1cm border. Brush border of pancakes with a little of the combined eggs and milk, fold into quarters. Coat pancakes with flour, shake off excess flour, dip pancakes in remaining egg mixture, then in combined breadcrumbs and sesame seeds. Refrigerate 30 minutes.

Just before serving, shallow-fry pancakes in hot oil until well browned on both sides; drain on absorbent paper.

Filling: Heat oils in pan, add shallots, cumin and anise, cook, stirring, until fragrant. Add mince, stir over heat until mince is well browned; remove and discard anise. Blend cornflour with water, sugar and sauce, add to mince mixture, stir over heat until mixture boils and thickens, stir in chestnuts, cool.

Pancakes: Sift flour into bowl, gradually stir in combined eggs, oil and milk, beat until smooth (or blend or process all ingredients until smooth); cover, stand 30 minutes. Pour 2 to 3 tablespoons of batter into heated greased heavy-based pan; cook until lightly browned underneath. Turn pancake, brown other side. Repeat with remaining batter. You will need 12 pancakes for this recipe.

Serves 6.

- Recipe can be prepared a day ahead.
- Storage: Covered, in refrigerator.
- Freeze: Uncooked parcels suitable.
- Microwave: Not suitable.

Clockwise from front: Crispy Pancakes with Water Chestnut Filling, Burghul and Potato Topped Bake, Piroshski.

Plates and napkin from Archway Tablewares.

BEEF RATATOUILLE AND FETA CREPES

1 cup plain flour
1 egg, lightly beaten
1¼ cups milk
2 teaspoons oil
2 tablespoons chopped fresh chives
350g feta cheese, crumbled

BEEF RATATOUILLE FILLING
1 tablespoon olive oil
2 cloves garlic, crushed
2 teaspoons paprika
300g minced beef
2 onions, chopped
1 tablespoon plain flour
1 large (about 250g) tomato, chopped
2 zucchini (about 200g), chopped
2 tablespoons tomato paste
1 tablespoon Worcestershire sauce
1 cup water

CHEESE SAUCE
200g packaged cream cheese, chopped
300ml cream

Sift flour into bowl, gradually stir in combined egg, milk and oil, beat until smooth; stir in chives; cover, stand 30 minutes.

Pour 2 to 3 tablespoons of batter into heated greased heavy-based pan, cook until lightly browned underneath, turn crepe, brown other side. Repeat with remaining batter. You will need 12 crepes for this recipe.

Fill crepes with beef ratatouille filling, roll up, place in single layer in greased ovenproof dish. Pour over cheese sauce, sprinkle with feta cheese, bake uncovered in moderately hot oven about 15 minutes or until heated through.

Beef Ratatouille Filling: Heat oil in pan, add garlic, paprika, mince and onions, stir over heat until mince is browned. Add flour, tomato and zucchini, stir until combined. Remove from heat, gradually stir in combined paste, sauce and water, stir over heat until mixture boils and thickens. Simmer, uncovered, until zucchini is tender; cool.

Cheese Sauce: Blend or process cheese and cream until smooth.

Serves 6.

- Crepes, filling and sauce can be prepared separately day ahead.
- Storage: Covered, in refrigerator.
- Freeze: Crepes and filling suitable.
- Microwave: Not suitable.

Clockwise from front: Beef Ratatouille and Feta Crepes, Tartlets with Beef and Corn, Tortellini with Sage Butter.

TARTLETS WITH BEEF AND CORN

12 slices bread
30g butter, softened
1 (about 130g) tomato, seeded, chopped
1 tablespoon chopped fresh coriander

BEEF AND CORN FILLING
1 tablespoon oil
1 onion, finely chopped
1 clove garlic, crushed
1 teaspoon ground cumin
500g minced beef
1 cup (180g) corn kernels
¼ teaspoon chilli powder
300g can Tomato Supreme
1 tablespoon chopped fresh coriander

Cut crusts from bread, roll bread slices with rolling pin until thin. Cut 9cm round from each slice of bread; spread 1 side of bread with butter. Place bread, buttered side down, into 2 greased 6-hole Texas muffin pans. Bake in moderately hot oven about 15 minutes or until lightly browned.

Just before serving, spoon filling evenly into bread cases, sprinkle with tomato and coriander, bake in moderate oven about 10 minutes or until heated through.

Beef and Corn Filling: Heat oil in pan, add onion, garlic and cumin, cook, stirring, until onion is soft. Add mince, stir over heat until browned. Add corn, chilli powder, Tomato Supreme and coriander, stir until well combined and heated through.

Serves 4.

- Recipe can be prepared a day ahead.
- Storage: Bread cases, in airtight container. Filling, covered, in refrigerator.
- Freeze: Filling suitable.
- Microwave: Filling suitable.

TORTELLINI WITH SAGE BUTTER

It is important to use 60g eggs in this recipe for tortellini.
125g butter, melted
2 tablespoons small sage leaves
grated fresh parmesan cheese

TORTELLINI
2 cups plain flour
3 eggs, lightly beaten

FILLING
300g minced beef
1 clove garlic, crushed
¼ cup grated fresh parmesan cheese
½ teaspoon cracked black peppercorns
½ small onion, chopped

Add tortellini to large pan of boiling water, simmer, uncovered, until just tender; drain. Place hot tortellini into large bowl; toss through combined butter and sage. Serve sprinkled with parmesan cheese.

Tortellini: Combine flour and eggs in

processor; process until mixture forms a ball. Knead dough on lightly floured surface until smooth. Cut dough in half, roll each half through pasta machine set on thickest setting. Fold dough in half, roll through machine. Repeat rolling and folding several times until dough is very smooth and elastic, dusting dough with a

little extra flour when necessary. Roll dough through machine, adjusting setting to become less thick with each roll. Roll to 1mm thickness (No.7 on pasta machine). Cut pasta into 8cm rounds; place a level teaspoon of filling in the centre of each round. Lightly brush edges of rounds with water, fold rounds in half; press edges together to seal. Pinch points together.

Filling: Process all ingredients until well combined.

Serves 4 to 6.

◼ Best made just before serving.
◼ Freeze: Uncooked tortellini suitable.
◼ Microwave: Suitable.

ZUCCHINI WITH WILD RICE SEASONING

⅓ cup wild rice
6 (about 600g) zucchini
1 tablespoon oil
1 onion, finely chopped
1 clove garlic, crushed
400g minced beef
1 tablespoon white vinegar
1 teaspoon curry powder
1 teaspoon sugar
1 (about 130g) tomato, seeded,
    chopped
¼ cup water
1 tablespoon packaged breadcrumbs

YOGURT SAUCE
1 cup plain yogurt
1 tablespoon lemon juice
1 tablespoon chopped fresh chives

Add rice to pan of boiling water, simmer, uncovered, about 30 minutes or until rice is tender; drain.

Cut zucchini in half lengthways, scoop out and discard seeds. Add zucchini to large pan of boiling water, boil, uncovered, 1 minute; drain, rinse under cold water; drain.

Heat oil in pan add onion and garlic, cook, stirring, until onion is soft. Add mince, stir over heat until mince is browned, add rice, vinegar, curry powder, sugar, tomato and water. Bring to boil, simmer, uncovered, 5 minutes; cool. Spoon filling into zucchini halves, place on oven tray; sprinkle with breadcrumbs. Bake, uncovered, in moderate oven about 10 minutes or until heated through. Serve zucchini with yogurt sauce.

Yogurt Sauce: Combine all ingredients in bowl; mix well.

Serves 4.

■ Recipe can be prepared a day ahead.
■ Storage: Covered, in refrigerator.
■ Freeze: Not suitable.
■ Microwave: Zucchini suitable.

MACARONI AND BEEF TOMATOES

6 (about 800g) tomatoes
250g minced beef
1 onion, finely chopped
1 clove garlic, crushed
2 tablespoons tomato paste
⅓ cup small macaroni
¾ cup water
1 small beef stock cube
⅓ cup stale breadcrumbs
¼ cup grated parmesan cheese
15g butter, melted

Cut a thin slice from top of each tomato. Scoop out flesh, leaving ½cm shell. Chop tomato flesh finely; reserve.

Heat pan, add mince, onion and garlic, stir over heat until mince is browned. Stir in reserved tomato flesh, paste, macaroni, water and crumbled stock cube. Bring to boil, simmer, uncovered, about 20 minutes or until mixture is thick and macaroni tender. Spoon mince mixture into tomato shells, place on oven tray. Combine breadcrumbs, cheese and butter in bowl, spoon over mince mixture. Bake, uncovered, in moderate oven about 25 minutes or until topping is browned.

Serves 6.

■ Recipe can be prepared a day ahead.
■ Storage: Covered, in refrigerator.
■ Freeze: Not suitable.
■ Microwave: Suitable.

SCOTCH EGGS WITH HERB MAYONNAISE

6 hard-boiled eggs
plain flour
500g sausage mince
1 egg, lightly beaten
1 tablespoon milk
⅔ cup packaged breadcrumbs
oil for deep-frying

HERB MAYONNAISE
1 egg
1 egg yolk
1 tablespoon lemon juice
1 cup oil
1 tablespoon chopped fresh chives
1 tablespoon chopped fresh oregano

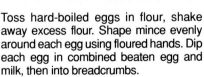

CHICKEN POTS WITH HERBED CHEESE SAUCE

2 bacon rashers, chopped
30g butter
250g minced chicken
1 teaspoon turmeric
2 teaspoons paprika
100g mushrooms, chopped
¼ cup plain flour
1 cup milk
3 eggs, lightly beaten
½ cup grated smoked cheese
⅓ cup grated smoked cheese, extra

HERBED CHEESE SAUCE
125g packet cream cheese
½ cup cream
¼ teaspoon dried thyme leaves
2 teaspoons shredded fresh basil
1 tablespoon chopped fresh parsley

Cook bacon in hot pan until crisp; drain on absorbent paper.

Heat butter in pan, add mince and spices, cook, stirring, until mince is well browned. Add mushrooms, cook, stirring, until mushrooms are soft. Remove from heat, stir in flour, then gradually stir in milk, stir over heat until mixture boils and thickens; cool.

Stir bacon, eggs and cheese into mixture. Divide mixture between 4 greased ovenproof dishes (1 cup capacity). Place dishes in baking dish with enough hot water to come halfway up sides of dishes. Bake, covered, in moderate oven about 45 minutes or until set. Stand 5 minutes before turning onto flameproof tray.

Just before serving, sprinkle pots with extra cheese, grill until lightly browned and heated through. Serve with hot herbed cheese sauce.

Herbed Cheese Sauce: Blend or process cheese and cream until smooth. Combine cheese mixture and herbs in pan, stir over heat until heated through.

Serves 4.

- Pots and sauce can be made a day ahead.
- Storage: Covered, in refrigerator.
- Freeze: Not suitable.
- Microwave: Sauce suitable.

LEFT: From left: Zucchini with Wild Rice Seasoning, Macaroni and Beef Tomatoes, Scotch Eggs with Herb Mayonnaise. BELOW: Chicken Pots with Herbed Cheese Sauce.

Above: Plate and fork from Limoges.

Toss hard-boiled eggs in flour, shake away excess flour. Shape mince evenly around each egg using floured hands. Dip each egg in combined beaten egg and milk, then into breadcrumbs.

Deep-fry eggs 1 at a time in hot oil until cooked through; drain on absorbent paper. Serve with herb mayonnaise.

Herb Mayonnaise: Blend or process egg, egg yolk and juice until smooth. With motor operating, gradually add oil in thin stream, blend until thickened; stir in herbs.

Makes 6.

- Recipe can be prepared 2 days ahead.
- Storage: Covered, in refrigerator.
- Freeze: Not suitable.
- Microwave: Not suitable.

SESAME BEEF ROLLS

1 tablespoon oil
3 green shallots, chopped
1 teaspoon ground cumin
½ teaspoon turmeric
¼ teaspoon chilli powder
300g minced beef
2 eggs, lightly beaten
¼ cup chopped fresh parsley
8 sheets fillo pastry
90g butter, melted
30g butter, melted, extra
1 tablespoon sesame seeds

Heat oil in pan, add shallots, cumin, turmeric and chilli powder, cook, stirring, until shallots are soft. Add mince, stir over heat until browned. Remove from heat, stir in eggs, stir until eggs are just beginning to set; cool. Stir in parsley.

Layer 2 sheets of pastry together, brushing each with butter. Cut pastry in half lengthways, cut each half into quarters. Place 2 level teaspoons of mince mixture onto long edge of 1 piece of pastry, roll up, tucking in ends, to form a thin roll. Repeat with remaining pastry, butter and filling. Place rolls on lightly greased oven trays; brush with extra butter, sprinkle with sesame seeds. Bake in moderately hot oven about 10 minutes or until browned.

Makes 32.

- Rolls can be prepared 3 hours ahead.
- Storage: Covered, in refrigerator.
- Freeze: Uncooked rolls suitable.
- Microwave: Filling suitable.

MINI MEATLOAVES WITH YOGURT SAUCE

1 bunch (40 leaves) English spinach
1 tablespoon oil
1 (about 120g) carrot, grated
1 (about 100g) zucchini, grated
1 stick celery, finely chopped
1 small red pepper, finely chopped
2 cloves garlic, crushed
400g can tomatoes
1 cup (70g) stale breadcrumbs
2 tablespoons currants
500g minced beef

YOGURT SAUCE
200g carton plain yogurt
2 teaspoons lemon juice
1 clove garlic, crushed
1 teaspoon cracked black
   peppercorns
2 green shallots, chopped
1 tablespoon shredded fresh basil

Lightly grease 8 mini loaf pans (¾ cup capacity). Add spinach to large pan of simmering water; simmer, uncovered, until spinach is wilted, rinse under cold water; drain, pat dry with absorbent paper. Line prepared pans with spinach leaves overhanging slightly.

Heat oil in pan, add carrot, zucchini, celery, pepper and garlic, cook, stirring, until vegetables are tender. Stir in undrained crushed tomatoes, bring to boil, simmer, uncovered, about 10 minutes or until liquid is evaporated and mixture is thick; cool. Add breadcrumbs, currants and mince to vegetable mixture; mix well.

Divide mince mixture between prepared pans; press firmly into pans. Fold overhanging spinach over mince, cover with greased foil. Place pans on oven tray, bake in moderate oven about 1 hour or until firm. Cool meatloaves, refrigerate several hours or overnight. Serve meatloaves with yogurt sauce.

Yogurt Sauce: Combine all ingredients in bowl; mix well.

Serves 8.

- Meatloaves best made a day ahead; sauce can be made a day ahead.
- Storage: Covered, in refrigerator.
- Freeze: Meatloaves suitable.
- Microwave: Spinach suitable.

HAM AND PORK TERRINE WITH CUMBERLAND SAUCE

60g butter
1 onion, chopped
1kg minced pork and veal
2 bacon rashers, chopped
½ cup port
2 eggs
2 cups (140g) stale breadcrumbs
¼ cup shredded fresh sage
6 slices round ham
6 baby mushrooms
1 egg, lightly beaten, extra

PASTRY
2 cups plain flour
1 cup self-raising flour
180g butter
2 tablespoons lemon juice
¼ cup water, approximately

CUMBERLAND SAUCE
1 lemon
2 oranges
2 tablespoons redcurrant jelly
¼ cup port
½ teaspoon French mustard
2 green shallots, chopped

Heat butter in pan, add onion, cook, stirring, until soft; cool. Process onion mixture, mince, bacon, port, egg and breadcrumbs until well combined, stir in sage. Press mixture into a 20cm x 35cm rectangle on baking paper. Cover with slices of ham. Place mushrooms at short end, roll up like a Swiss roll using paper as a guide. Place roll in lightly greased 14cm x 21cm loaf pan, seam side down. Cover with greased foil, bake in moderate oven, about 2 hours.

Turn terrine from pan; drain, stand 10 minutes. Return terrine to pan, cover with plastic wrap, place another pan on top, fill with weights; refrigerate overnight.

Roll pastry to 35cm square, brush with some of the extra egg. Place terrine in centre of pastry, cut away corners so

pastry looks like a large cross (see picture). Fold pastry over top of terrine to enclose terrine, trim edges neatly; pinch edges together firmly to seal.

Place on lightly greased oven tray, decorate with scraps of pastry. Brush pastry all over with more extra egg. Bake in moderately hot oven about 40 minutes or until lightly browned. Cool terrine to room temperature. Serve terrine sliced, with cumberland sauce.

Pastry: Sift flours into bowl, rub in butter. Add lemon juice and enough water to make ingredients cling together. Knead gently on lightly floured surface until smooth, cover, refrigerate 30 minutes.

Cumberland Sauce: Using a vegetable peeler, peel rind thinly from lemon and 1 of the oranges. Cut rind into thin strips. Place rind in pan, cover with water, bring to boil; boil, uncovered, 3 minutes; drain. Squeeze juice from lemon and both oranges; you will need 2 tablespoons lemon juice and ½ cup orange juice. Combine rind, juices, jelly, port and mustard in pan, bring to boil, simmer, 2 minutes, stir in shallots; cool.

Serves 8.

- Terrine can be made a week ahead.
- Storage: Covered, in refrigerator.
- Freeze: Not suitable.
- Microwave: Sauce suitable.

LEFT: From top: Mini Meatloaves with Yogurt Sauce, Sesame Beef Rolls.
BELOW: Ham and Pork Terrine with Cumberland Sauce.

MINT SAUSAGE AND RED CABBAGE SALAD

6 slices white bread
80g butter, melted
4 cups (about 400g) shredded
    red cabbage
1 green pepper, sliced
1 yellow pepper, sliced

MINT SAUSAGES
250g minced beef
2 eggs, lightly beaten
1½ cups (110g) stale breadcrumbs
1½ tablespoons chopped fresh mint
½ cup stale breadcrumbs, extra
1 tablespoon oil

DRESSING
100g Roquefort cheese, chopped
80g packaged cream cheese,
    chopped
⅓ cup cream
2 tablespoons white wine vinegar
1 tablespoon lemon juice
2 tablespoons oil

Remove crusts from bread, brush bread with butter, cut each slice into 8 triangles. Place on oven tray, bake in moderately hot oven about 10 minutes or until croutons are lightly browned.

Just before serving, combine croutons, cabbage, peppers and sliced sausages in serving bowl. Drizzle cabbage mixture with dressing.

Mint Sausages: Process mince, eggs, breadcrumbs and mint until well combined. Divide mixture into 4 portions, roll each into a 3cm thick sausage, roll sausages in extra breadcrumbs. Heat oil in pan, add sausages, cook until browned and cooked through; drain on absorbent paper, cool.
Dressing: Blend or process all ingredients until smooth.

Serves 4.
- Sausages and dressing can be made a day ahead.
- Storage: Covered, in refrigerator.
- Freeze: Sausages suitable.
- Microwave: Not suitable.

MEATBALLS IN BATTER WITH SWEET CHILLI SAUCE

400g minced beef
3 teaspoons brown sugar
1 tablespoon light soy sauce
1 teaspoon grated fresh ginger
1 tablespoon plain flour
2 teaspoons white vinegar
½ cup walnuts, finely chopped
plain flour, extra
oil for deep-frying

BATTER
½ cup plain flour
1 egg
½ cup soda water

SWEET CHILLI SAUCE
1 tablespoon light soy sauce
1 tablespoon white vinegar
½ teaspoon grated lemon rind
¼ cup brown sugar
½ cup water
1 small fresh red chilli, finely chopped

Combine mince, sugar, sauce, ginger, flour, vinegar and nuts in bowl; mix well. Shape 2 level teaspoons of mixture into balls. Toss meatballs in extra flour, shake away excess flour. Dip meatballs in batter, deep-fry in hot oil until browned and cooked through; drain. Serve meatballs with sweet chilli sauce.
Batter: Sift flour into bowl, gradually stir in combined egg and soda water; beat until smooth; cover, stand 30 minutes.
Sweet Chilli Sauce: Combine sauce, vinegar, rind, sugar and water in pan. Stir over heat, without boiling, until sugar is dissolved. Bring to boil, simmer, uncovered, 3 minutes; stir in chilli.

Makes about 50.
- Meatballs and sauce can be made a day ahead.
- Storage: Covered, in refrigerator.
- Freeze: Not suitable.
- Microwave: Not suitable.

SAVOURY BREAD ROLLS WITH CHEESY TOPPING

8 bread rolls
1½ cups (190g) grated tasty cheese

FILLING
1 tablespoon oil
1 onion, chopped
1 clove garlic, crushed
500g minced beef
1 green pepper, chopped
125g mushrooms, chopped
400g can tomatoes
50g packet cream of mushroom
    soup mix
2 tablespoons chopped fresh parsley

Cut top from each bread roll; discard tops. Press bread against crust to form a shell. Spoon filling into rolls, place on oven tray, sprinkle with cheese. Bake in moderately hot oven about 15 minutes or until cheese is melted.
Filling: Heat oil in pan, add onion and garlic, cook, stirring, until onion is soft. Add mince, stir over heat until mince is well browned. Add pepper, mushrooms, undrained crushed tomatoes, dry soup mix and parsley; stir over heat until mixture boils and thickens.

Makes 8.
- Filling can be prepared a day ahead.
- Storage: Covered, in refrigerator.
- Freeze: Filling suitable.
- Microwave: Not suitable.

MUSHROOM AND MINCE TRIANGLES

10 sheets fillo pastry
180g butter, melted

FILLING
½ cup (15g) dried
Chinese mushrooms
2 tablespoons oil
200g minced beef
1 clove garlic, crushed
2 teaspoons grated fresh ginger
½ small leek, sliced
125g mushrooms, sliced
100g ham, chopped
2 tablespoons port
1 teaspoon five spice powder

Layer 2 pastry sheets together, brushing each with some of the butter, cut crossways into 7cm strips. Spoon a level tablespoon of filling on 1 end of each strip. Fold ends over to form triangles, continue folding to end of strips, brush with more butter. Repeat with remaining pastry, filling and butter.

Place triangles onto lightly greased oven trays. Bake in moderately hot oven about 10 minutes or until lightly browned.
Filling: Place mushrooms in bowl, cover with boiling water; stand 20 minutes. Drain mushrooms, discard stems, chop caps. Heat oil in pan, add mince, garlic, ginger and leek, stir over heat until mince is well browned. Add both mushrooms, ham, port and spice. Bring to boil, simmer,

covered, stirring occasionally, about 30 minutes or until mince is tender; cool.

Makes about 30.

■ Recipe can be made 3 hours ahead.
■ Storage: Covered, in refrigerator.
■ Freeze: Uncooked triangles suitable.
■ Microwave: Not suitable.

ABOVE LEFT: Mint Sausage and Red Cabbage Salad.
ABOVE: Clockwise from left: Mushroom and Mince Triangles, Savoury Bread Rolls with Cheesy Topping, Meatballs in Batter with Sweet Chilli Sauce.

Above left: Plate from Made in Japan; tiles from Pazotti. Above: Plates from Amy's Tableware.

BEEF AND GINGER WONTONS

350g minced beef
230g can water chestnuts, drained,
    chopped
1 tablespoon chopped fresh
    coriander
2 teaspoons ground ginger
1 tablespoon dark soy sauce
½ teaspoon sesame oil
2 teaspoons cornflour
40 x 8cm square egg pastry sheets
oil for deep-frying

Combine mince, chestnuts, coriander, ginger, sauce, sesame oil and cornflour in bowl; mix well. Cover, refrigerate 1 hour.

Place 2 level teaspoons of mixture in centre of each pastry sheet, brush edges with water. Bring points together in centre, press edges firmly to seal.

Deep-fry wontons in hot oil until lightly browned and cooked through. Drain on absorbent paper. Serve immediately.

Makes 40.

- Can be prepared 3 hours ahead.
- Storage: Covered, in refrigerator.
- Freeze: Uncooked wontons suitable.
- Microwave: Not suitable.

CHILLI BEEF PANCAKES

400g minced beef
1 onion, finely chopped
1 green pepper, finely chopped
½ teaspoon chilli powder
½ teaspoon cumin seeds
410g can tomatoes
225g can baked beans in
    tomato sauce
2 tablespoons tomato paste
½ small lettuce, shredded
1 cup (125g) grated tasty cheese

PANCAKES
1 cup plain flour
1¼ cups milk
1 egg, lightly beaten

Stir mince, onion, pepper, chilli powder and cumin seeds in large pan over heat until mince is well browned. Stir in un-drained crushed tomatoes, beans and paste. Bring to boil, simmer, uncovered, about 25 minutes or until thick.

Spoon hot mixture over pancakes, top with lettuce, roll up, place in single layer in shallow flameproof dish, sprinkle with cheese, grill until melted.

Pancakes: Sift flour into bowl, gradually stir in combined milk and egg, beat until smooth. Pour ¼ cup batter into heated, greased, heavy-based pan; cook until lightly browned underneath. Turn pancake, brown other side. Repeat with remaining batter. You need 12 pancakes.

Serves 6.

- Pancakes and mince mixture can be made separately a day ahead.
- Storage: Covered, in refrigerator.
- Freeze: Unfilled pancakes suitable.
- Microwave: Not suitable.

PORK PIE

3 cups plain flour
2 egg yolks
125g lard, chopped
⅔ cup water
1 egg yolk, extra
1 tablespoon milk

FILLING
500g minced pork and veal
2 bacon rashers, chopped
1 tablespoon chopped fresh thyme
1 tablespoon chopped fresh sage

ASPIC
½ cup water
1 teaspoon beef stock powder
2 teaspoons gelatine
2 teaspoons cranberry sauce

Sift flour into bowl, add egg yolks, cover with some of the flour. Combine lard and water in pan, stir over heat until lard is melted, bring to boil, stir quickly into flour mixture, mix to a firm dough with wooden spoon. Turn dough onto lightly floured surface, knead lightly until smooth, cover, stand 10 minutes.

Knead pastry again until smooth. Roll two-thirds of pastry large enough to line base and side of greased deep 18cm round cake pan. Press pastry firmly into pan, making sure there are no cracks or holes, trim edge. Spread filling into pan.

Brush pastry edge with combined extra egg yolk and milk. Roll remaining pastry large enough to cover filling, press edges together. Cut 2cm hole in centre of pie, brush pastry with remaining egg mixture.

Bake pie in hot oven about 45 minutes or until golden brown, cover pan with foil, reduce heat to moderate, bake further 1 hour; cool in pan. Pour aspic through hole in pastry; refrigerate pie in pan overnight.

Filling: Combine all ingredients in bowl; mix well.

Aspic: Combine all ingredients in small pan, stir over low heat until gelatine is dissolved; cool slightly.

Serves 6 to 8.

- Recipe can be made 4 days ahead.
- Storage: Covered, in refrigerator.
- Freeze: Not suitable.
- Microwave: Aspic suitable.

LEFT: From top: Chilli Beef Pancakes, Beef and Ginger Wontons.
ABOVE: Pork Pie.

TOMATO SOUP WITH MEATBALLS AND PASTA

1 tablespoon olive oil
1 onion, chopped
2 cloves garlic, crushed
2 x 410g cans tomatoes
1½ tablespoons tomato paste
2 large beef stock cubes
1½ litres (6 cups) hot water
1 tablespoon sugar
⅓ cup small elbow pasta
2 tablespoons chopped fresh basil

MEATBALLS
500g minced beef
¾ cup stale breadcrumbs
1 onion, chopped
1 clove garlic, crushed
1 egg yolk
1 tablespoon chopped fresh basil
1 tablespoon olive oil

Heat oil in pan, add onion and garlic, cook, stirring, until onion is soft. Add undrained crushed tomatoes, paste, crumbled stock cubes, water and sugar. Bring to boil, simmer, covered, 15 minutes. Stir in pasta and meatballs, boil, uncovered, until pasta is tender; stir in basil.

Meatballs: Process mince, breadcrumbs, onion, garlic, egg yolk and basil until finely minced. Roll 2 level teaspoons of mixture into balls. Heat oil in pan, add meatballs, cook, until browned and cooked through; drain on absorbent paper.

Serves 6.

■ Recipe can be made a day ahead.
■ Storage: Covered, in refrigerator.
■ Freeze: Suitable.
■ Microwave: Not suitable.

- Recipe can be made a day ahead.
- Storage: Covered, in refrigerator.
- Freeze: Suitable.
- Microwave: Not suitable.

SPINACH AND CHICKEN TERRINE WITH PEPPER SAUCE

**4 spinach (silverbeet) leaves
1 small red pepper
1 chicken breast fillet, sliced
450g minced chicken
¼ teaspoon ground nutmeg
¼ teaspoon paprika
2 tablespoons cream
2 tablespoons dry sherry
2 tablespoons pistachios**

PEPPER SAUCE
**1 red pepper, chopped
1 clove garlic, crushed
2 egg yolks
1 cup olive oil**

Remove stalks from spinach. Cut pepper into thin strips. Add spinach and pepper to pan of boiling water, drain immediately, rinse under cold water; drain well.

Reserve 1 spinach leaf. Line base and sides of lightly greased 8cm x 26cm bar cake pan with remaining spinach, leaving 2cm overhanging.

Wrap red pepper and chicken slices in reserved spinach leaf. Process mince, nutmeg, paprika, cream and sherry until well combined. Transfer mince mixture to bowl, stir in nuts.

Press half the mince mixture over base of lined pan, press spinach roll into centre of mixture, top with remaining mince mixture; press down firmly. Fold spinach leaves over to cover mince mixture; cover pan with foil.

Place pan in baking dish, pour in enough boiling water to come halfway up sides of pan. Bake in moderate oven about 1 hour or until firm; cool.

Refrigerate 3 hours or overnight before serving. Serve terrine with pepper sauce.
Pepper Sauce: Blend or process pepper, garlic and yolks until smooth. Add olive oil gradually in a thin stream while motor is operating.

- Recipe can be made 2 days ahead.
- Storage: Covered, in refrigerator.
- Freeze: Not suitable.
- Microwave: Not suitable.

OLIVE MINCE BREAD

**7g sachet granulated yeast
1 teaspoon sugar
½ cup warm water
3 cups plain flour
1 tablespoon olive oil
¾ cup warm water, approximately, extra
1 tablespoon olive oil, extra
2 onions, thinly sliced
¾ cup black olives, chopped
1 egg yolk, lightly beaten
½ teaspoon dried oregano leaves
½ teaspoon dried basil leaves**

MINCE FILLING
**1 tablespoon olive oil
2 cloves garlic, crushed
500g minced beef
400g can tomatoes
2 tablespoons tomato paste
2 tablespoons chopped fresh basil**

Combine yeast, sugar and water in small bowl. Cover, stand in warm place about 10 minutes or until mixture is frothy.

Sift flour into large bowl, stir in yeast mixture, oil and enough extra water to form a soft dough. Turn dough onto floured surface, knead about 8 minutes or until smooth and elastic. Return dough to large greased bowl, cover, stand in warm place about 30 minutes or until dough is doubled in size.

Meanwhile, heat extra oil in pan, add onions, cook, stirring, until soft.

Turn dough onto lightly floured surface, knead until smooth. Divide dough in half, roll each half to 20cm x 30cm rectangle. Place half into greased 20cm x 30cm lamington pan. Top dough with mince filling, then onions and olives, then the remaining dough. Pierce dough at 3cm intervals with skewer, stand, uncovered, in warm place about 30 minutes or until dough is risen above top of pan.

Brush dough with yolk, sprinkle with herbs. Bake in moderately hot oven 15 minutes, reduce heat to moderate, bake further 10 minutes or until browned. Turn onto wire rack, cool before cutting.
Mince Filling: Heat oil in pan, add garlic and mince, stir over heat until mince is browned. Add undrained crushed tomatoes, paste and basil, simmer, uncovered, until liquid is evaporated.

FAR LEFT: From top: Olive Mince Bread, Tomato Soup with Meatballs and Pasta.
ABOVE LEFT: Spinach and Chicken Terrine with Pepper Sauce.

Above left: Tiles from Country Floors; plate and fork from Limoges.

CHILLI RAVIOLI WITH CREAMY TOMATO SAUCE

It is important to use 60g eggs in this recipe for ravioli.

2 cups plain flour
2 eggs
2 tablespoons olive oil
2 tablespoons water

FILLING
1 tablespoon olive oil
1 small red Spanish onion, finely chopped
1 clove garlic, crushed
300g minced beef
1 teaspoon sambal oelek
1 tablespoon tomato paste
1 teaspoon dried basil leaves
1 small beef stock cube

CREAMY TOMATO SAUCE
2 x 410g cans tomatoes
1 small beef stock cube
1 clove garlic, crushed
1 tablespoon cornflour
¼ cup water
½ cup sour cream
1 tablespoon chopped fresh parsley

Sift flour into bowl, stir in eggs, oil and water; mix to a soft dough (or blend or process all ingredients until combined). Turn dough onto lightly floured surface, knead about 10 minutes or until smooth and elastic. Cover, stand 20 minutes.

Divide dough in half, roll each half on floured surface to 1mm thickness (No. 7 on pasta machine). Place level teaspoons of filling at 3cm intervals over half the dough, brush a little water lightly between fillings. Top with remaining dough, press firmly between fillings and along edges. Cut into squares with pastry wheel. Sprinkle ravioli with a little extra flour.

Add ravioli to large pan of boiling water just before serving. Boil, uncovered, about 5 minutes or until ravioli is just tender; drain. Serve ravioli with creamy tomato sauce.

Filling: Heat oil in pan, add onion and garlic, cook, stirring, until onion is soft. Add mince, stir over heat until browned, simmer, uncovered, until liquid is evaporated. Stir in sambal oelek, paste, basil and crumbled stock cube.

Creamy Tomato Sauce: Blend or process undrained crushed tomatoes until smooth. Combine tomatoes in pan with crumbled stock cube, garlic and blended cornflour and water. Stir over heat until sauce boils and thickens; stir in sour cream and parsley.

Serves 6.

- Recipe can be prepared a day ahead.
- Storage: Covered, in refrigerator.
- Freeze: Uncooked ravioli suitable.
- Microwave: Sauce suitable.

CORN AND CHICKEN FRITTERS

2 eggs, lightly beaten
200g minced chicken
440g can corn kernels, drained
3 green shallots, chopped
1 tablespoon chopped fresh parsley
2 tablespoons chopped fresh coriander
1 tablespoon light soy sauce
2 tablespoons cornflour
1 teaspoon sugar
oil for shallow-frying

Combine eggs, mince, corn, shallots, herbs, sauce, cornflour and sugar in bowl; cover, mix well, refrigerate 30 minutes.

Just before serving, heat oil in pan, add ¼ cup of mixture to pan, cook on both sides until lightly browned and cooked through; drain on absorbent paper. Repeat with remaining mixture.

Makes 8.

- Recipe can be prepared 3 hours ahead.
- Storage: Covered, in refrigerator.
- Freeze: Not suitable.
- Microwave: Not suitable.

LEFT: Chilli Ravioli with Creamy Tomato Sauce.
ABOVE RIGHT: From back: Curried Chicken and Zucchini Soup, Corn and Chicken Fritters.

CURRIED CHICKEN AND ZUCCHINI SOUP

80g butter
1 onion, chopped
2 teaspoons curry powder
500g minced chicken
1/3 cup plain flour
1 litre (4 cups) water
2 large chicken stock cubes
2 (about 200g) zucchini, grated

Heat butter in pan, add onion and curry powder, cook, stirring, until onion is soft. Add mince, cook, stirring, until mince changes colour. Add flour, cook, stirring, 1 minute; add water and crumbled stock cubes, bring to boil, simmer, uncovered, 5 minutes.

Transfer mixture to bowl, cool. Cover soup, refrigerate several hours or overnight. Remove fat from soup, return soup to pan, bring to boil, add zucchini, stir over heat until heated through.

Serves 6.

■ Soup can be prepared a day ahead.
■ Storage: Covered, in refrigerator.
■ Freeze: Suitable.
■ Microwave: Suitable.

SUPREME COTTAGE LOAF

1 (about 300g) eggplant, sliced
coarse cooking salt
2 tablespoons olive oil
2 tablespoons olive oil, extra
1 onion, chopped
2 cloves garlic, crushed
500g minced lamb
400g can tomatoes
1 (25cm) round cottage loaf
1 cup (100g) grated mozzarella
    cheese
1 cup (125g) black olives, halved
½ cup chopped sun-dried tomatoes
¼ cup shredded fresh basil,
    firmly packed
¼ cup grated fresh parmesan cheese
1¼ cups (250g) ricotta cheese

Sprinkle eggplant with salt, stand 30 minutes. Rinse eggplant under cold water, pat dry with absorbent paper. Brush eggplant with oil, grill both sides of eggplant until lightly browned.

Heat extra oil in pan, add onion, garlic and mince; stir over heat until mince is browned. Stir in undrained crushed tomatoes, bring to boil, simmer, uncovered, about 10 minutes or until liquid is evaporated and mixture is thick.

Slice top from loaf, hollow out base of loaf to leave 2cm shell. Press mince mixture into base of loaf; top with mozzarella cheese, olives, sun-dried tomatoes, basil and eggplant. Sprinkle with parmesan cheese, top with ricotta cheese. Replace top of loaf.

Wrap loaf firmly in foil, place on oven tray, bake in moderate oven about 45 minutes or until heated through.

Serves 6.

- Recipe can be made 3 hours ahead.
- Storage: Covered, in refrigerator.
- Freeze: Suitable.
- Microwave: Not suitable.

CHICKEN TACOS WITH TOMATO SALSA

8 taco shells
4 lettuce leaves, shredded
1 avocado, mashed

FILLING
1 tablespoon oil
4 green shallots, chopped
500g minced chicken
1 teaspoon ground cumin
¼ teaspoon chilli powder
2 small chicken stock cubes
½ cup sour cream

TOMATO SALSA
2 large (about 500g) tomatoes,
    peeled, seeded
1 small onion, chopped
1 teaspoon sugar
1 teaspoon white vinegar

Heat tacos according to instructions on packet. Spoon filling into tacos, top with lettuce, tomato salsa and avocado.

Filling: Heat oil in pan, add shallots and mince, stir over heat until mince changes colour. Stir in cumin, chilli and crumbled stock cubes, cook, stirring, 1 minute. Stir in sour cream, cook, stirring, about 2 minutes or until thick.

Tomato Salsa: Combine all ingredients in bowl; mix well.

Makes 8.

- Filling and salsa can be prepared a day ahead.
- Storage: Covered, in refrigerator.
- Freeze: Not suitable.
- Microwave: Taco shells suitable.

KUMARA CHICKEN MEATBALLS WITH CRANBERRY SAUCE

300g kumara
1 tablespoon oil
1 small onion, finely chopped
1 clove garlic, crushed
500g minced chicken
1¼ cups (90g) stale breadcrumbs
½ teaspoon ground cinnamon
1 egg, lightly beaten
plain flour
3 eggs, lightly beaten, extra
1 cup (100g) packaged breadcrumbs
oil for deep-frying

CRANBERRY SAUCE
⅔ cup cranberry sauce
¼ cup water
1 teaspoon grated orange rind
2 green shallots, chopped

Boil, steam or microwave kumara until tender; drain, mash.

Heat oil in pan, add onion and garlic, cook, stirring, until onion is soft. Add mince, stir over heat until mince changes colour; drain, cool.

Combine mince mixture, kumara, stale breadcrumbs, cinnamon and egg in bowl; mix well, refrigerate 1 hour.

Shape 2 level teaspoons of mixture into balls. Toss meatballs in flour, shake away excess flour. Dip into extra eggs, toss in packaged breadcrumbs. Deep-fry meatballs in batches until browned; drain on absorbent paper. Serve meatballs with cranberry sauce.

Cranberry Sauce: Combine all ingredients in bowl; mix well.

Makes about 60.

- Recipe can be prepared 3 hours ahead.
- Storage: Covered, in refrigerator.
- Freeze: Meatballs suitable.
- Microwave: Kumara suitable.

MUSTARD CHICKEN JAFFLES

60g butter
8 slices thick white bread

FILLING
1 tablespoon oil
250g minced chicken
3 teaspoons seeded mustard
¾ cup grated tasty cheese
¼ cup sour cream
1 tablespoon chopped fresh chives

Spread butter over 1 side of each slice of bread. Place 4 slices of bread buttered side down on board, top evenly with filling; top with remaining bread, buttered side up. Toast in jaffle iron or sandwich maker until golden brown.

Filling: Heat oil in pan, add mince, stir over heat until mince changes colour, drain. Combine mince, mustard, cheese, cream and chives in bowl; mix well.

Makes 4.

■ Filling can be made 3 hours ahead.
■ Storage: Covered, in refrigerator.
■ Freeze: Not suitable.
■ Microwave: Filling suitable.

LEFT: Supreme Cottage Loaf.
ABOVE: From back: Kumara Chicken Meatballs with Cranberry Sauce, Chicken Tacos with Tomato Salsa, Mustard Chicken Jaffles.

Above: Tiles from Country Floors; plates from Villa Italiana.

37

DEEP DISH PIE WITH SMOKED CHEESE TOPPING

½ cup self-raising flour
1½ cups plain flour
125g butter
1 egg yolk
⅓ cup water, approximately
2 eggs, lightly beaten
¼ cup milk
1⅓ cups (150g) grated smoked cheese
paprika

FILLING
2 teaspoons olive oil
2 onions, finely chopped
2 cloves garlic, crushed
500g minced beef
¼ cup plain flour
425g can tomato puree
1 tablespoon chopped fresh oregano
1 tablespoon chopped fresh parsley
1 egg white, lightly beaten

Sift flours into bowl, rub in butter, add yolk and enough water to make ingredients cling together. Press dough into a ball, knead on floured surface until smooth, cover, refrigerate 30 minutes.

Roll dough on lightly floured surface large enough to line greased 20cm springform tin, ease into tin, trim edge. Place tin on oven tray, line pastry with paper, fill with dried beans or rice, bake in moderately hot oven 20 minutes, remove paper and beans, bake further 20 minutes or until browned, cool.

Spoon filling into pastry shell, pour over combined eggs, milk and cheese. Sprinkle with paprika.

Bake in moderately hot oven 15 minutes, reduce heat to moderate, bake further 30 minutes or until top is set.
Filling: Heat oil in pan, add onion and garlic, cook, stirring, until onion is soft, add mince, stir over heat until mince is changed in colour.

Add flour, stir until combined. Remove pan from heat, gradually stir in puree and herbs, stir over heat 3 minutes or until mixture is thick; cool. Stir in egg white.

Serves 6.

■ Recipe best made 3 hours ahead.
■ Storage: Covered, in refrigerator.
■ Freeze: Not suitable.
■ Microwave: Filling suitable.

TARRAGON BEEF BURGERS WITH ONION SAUCE

10g butter
1 onion, finely chopped
2 cloves garlic, crushed
300g minced beef
1¼ cups (90g) stale breadcrumbs
1 egg, lightly beaten
1 tablespoon chopped fresh tarragon
2 tablespoons oil

ONION SAUCE
10g butter
1 onion, finely chopped
1 teaspoon white vinegar
300g carton sour cream
1 tablespoon chopped fresh parsley

Heat butter in pan, add onion and garlic, cook, stirring, until onion is soft; cool. Combine onion mixture, mince, breadcrumbs, egg and tarragon in bowl;

mix well. Shape mixture into 6 burgers, place on tray, cover; refrigerate 30 minutes. Heat oil in pan, add burgers, cook until well browned and tender. Serve burgers with onion sauce.

Onion Sauce: Heat butter in pan, add onion, cook, stirring, until soft. Add vinegar, cook 1 minute. Stir in sour cream, bring to boil, simmer, uncovered, until slightly thickened; stir in parsley.

Serves 4 to 6.

- Burgers can be prepared a day ahead.
- Storage: Covered, in refrigerator.
- Freeze: Uncooked burgers suitable.
- Microwave: Sauce suitable.

LAMB AND VEGETABLE PILLOWS

3 cups plain flour
1 teaspoon salt
60g butter
⅔ cup water, approximately
oil for deep-frying

FILLING
1 small (about 100g) potato, finely chopped
1 tablespoon oil
1 small onion, chopped
1 clove garlic, crushed
½ teaspoon grated fresh ginger
125g minced lamb
½ teaspoon ground cumin
1 teaspoon ground coriander
¼ teaspoon turmeric
¼ teaspoon garam masala
1 teaspoon chicken stock powder
¼ cup frozen peas
2 tablespoons water
1 teaspoon chopped fresh coriander

Sift flour and salt into bowl, rub in butter. Stir in enough water to make mixture cling together. Press dough into ball, knead gently on lightly floured surface until smooth, cover, refrigerate 30 minutes.

Roll half the dough on lightly floured surface until 2mm thick, cut 8cm rounds from dough. Repeat with remaining dough. Place level teaspoons of filling on each round, brush edges with water, fold rounds in half, press edges together.

Deep-fry pillows in hot oil until browned; drain on absorbent paper.

Filling: Boil, steam or microwave potato until tender. Heat oil in pan, add onion, garlic and ginger, cook, stirring, until onion is soft. Add mince, spices and stock powder. Stir over heat until mince is browned, add peas and water. Bring to boil, simmer, uncovered, until peas are tender, stir in potato and coriander.

Makes about 40.

- Filling can be made a day ahead.
- Storage: Covered, in refrigerator.
- Freeze: Not suitable.
- Microwave: Filling suitable.

MEATBALLS WITH CORN AND CARAWAY DIPS

500g minced lamb
1 onion, chopped
2 cloves garlic, crushed
1 teaspoon beef stock powder
1½ cups (110g) stale breadcrumbs
1 egg, lightly beaten
2 tablespoons oil

CORN DIP
2 teaspoons oil
2 cloves garlic, crushed
1 small red pepper, finely chopped
1 teaspoon ground cumin
½ teaspoon ground coriander
½ teaspoon garam masala
1 teaspoon sambal oelek
310g can creamed corn
1 tablespoon chopped fresh coriander

CARAWAY DIP
3 teaspoons caraway seeds
¾ cup sour cream

Process mince, onion, garlic, stock powder, breadcrumbs and egg until fine. Roll 2 level teaspoons of mixture into balls. Heat oil in pan, add meatballs, cook, until browned and tender; drain on absorbent paper. Serve with warm dips.

Corn Dip: Heat oil in pan, add garlic and pepper, cook, stirring, until pepper is soft. Add spices, cook 1 minute. Stir in corn; heat through; stir in coriander.

Caraway Dip: Heat seeds in dry pan, stir over heat until seeds begin to pop; add cream, stir until heated through.

Makes about 60.

- Recipe can be made a day ahead.
- Storage: Covered, in refrigerator.
- Freeze: Meatballs suitable.
- Microwave: Not suitable.

LEFT: From left: Deep Dish Pie with Smoked Cheese Topping, Tarragon Beef Burgers with Onion Sauce.

ABOVE: From top: Meatballs with Corn and Caraway Dips, Lamb and Vegetable Pillows.

Above: Plates from Corso de Fiori.

LAMB AND POTATO SALAD

5 large (about 1kg) potatoes, peeled, chopped
2 cups firmly packed watercress sprigs
1 tablespoon sesame seeds, toasted

MEATBALLS
500g minced lamb
2 tablespoons chopped fresh mint
½ cup stale breadcrumbs
1 egg, lightly beaten
2 tablespoons sesame seeds, toasted
cornflour
oil for shallow-frying

MAYONNAISE DRESSING
1 tablespoon oil
1 onion, sliced
1 cup mayonnaise
2 tablespoons white vinegar
⅓ cup water

Boil, steam or microwave potatoes until just tender; drain, cool. Combine potatoes, meatballs and mayonnaise dressing in bowl.

Add watercress, toss lightly to combine. Sprinkle with sesame seeds.

Meatballs: Combine mince, mint, breadcrumbs, egg and sesame seeds in bowl.

Roll 2 level teaspoons of mixture into balls; roll meatballs in cornflour. Shallow-fry meatballs in hot oil until well browned; drain on absorbent paper, cool.

Mayonnaise Dressing: Heat oil in pan, add onion, cook, stirring, until soft; cool. Combine onion mixture with remaining ingredients in bowl; mix well.

Serves 4 to 6.

■ Meatballs and mayonnaise dressing can be prepared a day ahead.
■ Storage: Covered, in refrigerator.
■ Freeze: Not suitable.
■ Microwave: Potatoes suitable.

40

FILLO ROLLS WITH TOMATO SAUCE

1 tablespoon oil
1 onion, finely chopped
450g minced lamb
1 clove garlic, crushed
1 teaspoon ground cinnamon
½ teaspoon ground allspice
¼ teaspoon ground ginger
pinch cayenne pepper
400g can tomatoes
1 tablespoon chopped fresh coriander
12 sheets fillo pastry
125g butter, melted

TOMATO SAUCE
1 tablespoon oil
1 green shallot, chopped
1 clove garlic, crushed
4 (about 500g) tomatoes, peeled, chopped
2 green shallots, chopped, extra

Heat oil in pan, add onion, cook, stirring, until soft, add mince and garlic, cook, stirring, until mince is well browned. Add spices, undrained crushed tomatoes and coriander. Bring to boil, simmer, covered, about 30 minutes or until thick; remove from heat, cool.

Layer 3 pastry sheets together, brushing each with butter, cut into 3 strips about 16cm x 29cm. Place 2 level tablespoons of mixture along short edge of each strip. Roll up, tucking ends in, to form a parcel. Repeat with remaining pastry, butter and filling. Place parcels on lightly greased oven tray, brush with remaining butter. Bake in moderately hot oven, about 15 minutes or until lightly browned. Serve with tomato sauce.

Tomato Sauce: Heat oil in pan, add shallot and garlic, cook, stirring, until shallot is soft. Add tomatoes, bring to boil, simmer, uncovered, until liquid is evaporated; stir in extra shallots.

Serves 4 to 6.

- Tomato sauce can be made a day ahead.
- Storage: Covered, in refrigerator.
- Freeze: Not suitable.
- Microwave: Tomato sauce suitable.

GROUND LAMB WITH PINE NUTS AND WITLOF

2 teaspoons oil
500g minced lamb
2 cloves garlic, crushed
1 onion, chopped
½ cup pine nuts
1 teaspoon sambal oelek
½ teaspoon grated fresh ginger
230g can sliced water chestnuts, drained, chopped
4 green shallots, chopped
2 teaspoons cornflour
½ cup water
1 tablespoon dry sherry
2 tablespoons light soy sauce
½ teaspoon sesame oil
1 small chicken stock cube
4 small witlof

Heat oil in pan, add mince, garlic, onion and nuts, stir over heat until mince is browned. Stir in sambal oelek, ginger, chestnuts and shallots, cook 2 minutes. Stir in blended cornflour and water, sherry, sauce, sesame oil and crumbled stock cube, stir over heat until mixture boils and thickens slightly.

Separate witlof leaves; spoon mince mixture onto leaves to serve.

Serves 4 to 6.

- Recipe can be prepared a day ahead.
- Storage: Covered, in refrigerator.
- Freeze: Mince mixture suitable.
- Microwave: Suitable.

FAR LEFT: From back: Lamb and Potato Salad, Fillo Rolls with Tomato Sauce.
LEFT: Ground Lamb with Pine Nuts and Witlof.

CHICKEN PASTIES

2 sheets ready-rolled puff pastry
1 egg, lightly beaten

FILLING
150g kumara
200g minced chicken
1 small onion, finely chopped
¼ teaspoon dried thyme leaves
¼ teaspoon dried sage leaves

Cut 2 x 12cm rounds from each sheet of pastry. Place a quarter of filling in centre of each round, brush edges with a little water, fold edges of pastry into centre, pinch edges together to seal. Place on lightly greased oven trays, brush with egg. Bake in moderate oven about 30 minutes or until browned.
Filling: Cut kumara into 1cm cubes. Boil, steam or microwave until just tender; cool. Combine kumara, mince, onion and herbs in bowl; mix well.

Makes 4.

- Recipe can be made 2 days ahead.
- Storage: Covered, in refrigerator.
- Freeze: Uncooked pasties suitable.
- Microwave: Kumara suitable.

PRAWN AND CHICKEN POUCHES WITH CHILLI SAUCE

1 tablespoon oil
1 small onion, finely chopped
1 clove garlic, crushed
½ stick celery, finely chopped
2 teaspoons grated fresh ginger
100g minced chicken
1 small (about 80g) carrot, finely chopped
125g cooked prawns, shelled, finely chopped
2 green shallots, chopped
½ teaspoon sesame oil
1 tablespoon light soy sauce
1 tablespoon dry sherry
¼ teaspoon sugar
40 wonton wrappers
1 egg, lightly beaten
oil for deep-frying

CHILLI SAUCE
½ cup water
¼ cup white vinegar
1 teaspoon hoi sin sauce
¼ teaspoon sambal oelek
½ cup brown sugar, firmly packed

Heat oil in pan, add onion, garlic and celery, cook, stirring, until onion is soft. Stir in ginger and mince, stir over heat until mince changes colour. Stir in carrot, prawns and shallots, cook, stirring, 2 minutes. Stir in sesame oil, sauce, sherry and sugar, stir until combined; cool.

Brush wonton wrappers with egg, top with level teaspoons of mince mixture. Pull up edges of pastry around mixture, pinch edges together to seal.

Deep-fry pouches in hot oil, in batches, until browned; drain on absorbent paper. Serve pouches with chilli sauce.

Chilli Sauce: Combine all ingredients in pan, stir over heat, without boiling, until sugar is dissolved. Bring to boil, simmer, uncovered, about 5 minutes or until slightly thickened. Top with a little chopped fresh red chilli, if desired.

Makes 40.

- Recipe can be prepared 3 hours ahead.
- Storage: Covered, in refrigerator.
- Freeze: Uncooked pouches suitable.
- Microwave: Not suitable.

CHICKEN MEATBALLS IN CREAMY TARRAGON SAUCE

500g minced chicken
250g chicken livers, chopped
2 cups (140g) stale breadcrumbs
1 onion, chopped
1 clove garlic, crushed
1 tablespoon chopped fresh tarragon
plain flour
oil for deep-frying

CREAMY TARRAGON SAUCE
50g butter
¼ cup plain flour
¼ cup tarragon vinegar
½ cup dry white wine
1 teaspoon chicken stock powder
¾ cup water
½ cup cream
1 tablespoon chopped fresh tarragon

Process mince, livers, breadcrumbs, onion, garlic and tarragon until well combined. Transfer mixture to bowl, cover, refrigerate 30 minutes.

Roll level tablespoons of mixture into balls with floured hands. Deep-fry meatballs until browned and cooked through; drain on absorbent paper.
Creamy Tarragon Sauce: Melt butter in pan, add flour, cook until bubbling. Remove from heat, gradually stir in vinegar, wine, stock powder, water, cream and tarragon; stir over heat until mixture boils and thickens. Add meatballs to sauce, cook until heated through.

Serves 6.

- Meatballs can be made a day ahead.
- Storage: Covered, in refrigerator.
- Freeze: Uncooked meatballs suitable.
- Microwave: Not suitable.

Clockwise from back left: Prawn and Chicken Pouches with Chilli Sauce, Chicken Pasties, Chicken Meatballs in Creamy Tarragon Sauce.

Plates from Villa Italiana.

CREPES WITH LAMB AND BLACK BEAN

1¼ cups plain flour
1 tablespoon chopped fresh
　coriander
1 egg
1½ cups milk
FILLING
500g minced lamb
2 tablespoons black bean sauce
1 tablespoon dark soy sauce
1 tablespoon sweet chilli sauce
2 tablespoons rice vinegar
3 teaspoons brown sugar
2 cloves garlic, crushed
½ teaspoon grated fresh ginger
2 tablespoons oil
6 green shallots, sliced
1 tablespoon cornflour
3 teaspoons water

Sift flour into bowl, gradually stir in combined coriander, egg and milk; stir until
smooth, cover, stand 30 minutes.

Pour 2 to 3 tablespoons of batter into
heated, greased heavy-based pan, cook
until lightly browned underneath; turn
crepe, brown on other side. Repeat with
remaining batter. You will need 12 crepes
for this recipe. Spread filling evenly over
crepes, fold into quarters to serve.
Filling: Combine mince, sauces, vinegar,
sugar, garlic and ginger in bowl; mix well.
Cover, stand 30 minutes.

Heat oil in pan, add mince mixture, stir
over heat until mince is browned. Add
shallots, stir over heat further 1 minute.
Stir in blended cornflour and water, stir
over heat until mixture boils and thickens.

Serves 4 to 6.

- ■ Recipe can be prepared a day ahead.
- ■ Storage: Covered, in refrigerator.
- ■ Freeze: Crepes and filling suitable,
　separately.
- ■ Microwave: Not suitable.

LAMB AND RICE DUMPLINGS IN LEMON SOUP

250g minced lamb
2 tablespoons rice
1 small onion, grated
1 clove garlic, crushed
1 tablespoon chopped fresh parsley
1 tablespoon chopped fresh mint
1 egg, lightly beaten
1 cup (100g) packaged breadcrumbs
1¾ litres (7 cups) water
1 large (about 250g) tomato, seeded,
　chopped
1 teaspoon lemon pepper seasoning
1 egg yolk
3 teaspoons plain flour
¼ cup lemon juice
4 green shallots, chopped

Combine mince, rice, onion, garlic, herbs,
egg and breadcrumbs in bowl; mix well.
Shape 2 level teaspoons of mixture into
balls. Combine water, tomato and pepper

in pan. Bring to boil, add mince dumplings, simmer, covered, 30 minutes or until
dumplings are cooked through; cool.

Blend egg yolk, flour and juice in bowl,
stir in 1 cup soup stock; stir into soup in
pan. Add shallots, stir over heat, without
boiling, until slightly thickened.

Serves 4.

- ■ Can be prepared 3 hours ahead.
- ■ Storage: Covered, in refrigerator.
- ■ Freeze: Not suitable.
- ■ Microwave: Not suitable.

*ABOVE: From left: Crepes with Lamb and
Black Bean, Lamb and Rice Dumplings in
Lemon Soup.
RIGHT: From back: Spinach Pots with Green
Peppercorn Sauce, Chicken and Tomato
Rolls with Sesame Mayonnaise*

*Above: China from Wedgwood. Right: China from
Limoges.*

CHICKEN AND TOMATO ROLLS WITH SESAME MAYONNAISE

90g rice vermicelli
250g minced chicken
2 tablespoons light soy sauce
2 tablespoons sweet chilli sauce
1 teaspoon dried oregano leaves
2 tablespoons chopped sun-dried tomatoes
32 spring roll pastry sheets
oil for deep-frying

SESAME MAYONNNAISE
1 cup mayonnaise
3 drops sesame oil
2 teaspoons sesame seeds, toasted

Cover vermicelli with hot water in bowl, stand 10 minutes; drain well.

Combine vermicelli, mince, sauces, oregano and tomatoes in bowl; mix well. Place level tablespoons of mince mixture on corner of each pastry sheet, brush edges with water. Fold left and right corners inwards, then bottom corner inwards. Roll pastry sheet to enclose filling. Deep-fry rolls in hot oil until lightly browned; drain on absorbent paper. Serve hot rolls with sesame mayonnaise.

Sesame Mayonnaise: Combine all ingredients in bowl; mix well.

Makes 32.

- Filling can be prepared 3 hours ahead.
- Storage: Covered, in refrigerator.
- Freeze: Uncooked rolls suitable.
- Microwave: Not suitable.

SPINACH POTS WITH GREEN PEPPERCORN SAUCE

6 spinach (silverbeet) leaves
⅓ cup rice
30g butter
1 clove garlic, crushed
1 teaspoon cumin seeds
250g minced chicken
1 teaspoon lemon pepper seasoning
2 teaspoons plain flour
⅓ cup water
1 small chicken stock cube
125g packet cream cheese, chopped
2 tablespoons chopped fresh mint
1 teaspoon dried thyme leaves
⅓ cup stale breadcrumbs
1 egg, lightly beaten

GREEN PEPPERCORN SAUCE
1 cup dry white wine
1 tablespoon lemon juice
2 teaspoons canned green peppercorns, rinsed, drained
200g butter, chopped

Remove stalks from spinach. Add spinach to pan of boiling water, drain immediately, rinse under cold water, drain; pat dry with absorbent paper.

Grease 6 ovenproof dishes (1 cup capacity); line with spinach leaves, allowing ends to overhang sides. Add rice to pan of boiling water, boil, uncovered, about 8 minutes or until just tender; drain.

Heat butter in pan, add garlic, seeds and mince, stir over heat until mince changes colour. Add pepper and flour, stir until combined. Remove from heat, gradually stir in water, crumbled stock cube and cheese, stir over heat until mixture boils and thickens. Stir in rice, herbs, breadcrumbs and egg.

Spoon chicken mixture evenly into lined dishes, fold spinach leaves over to cover mince mixture; cover with foil.

Place dishes in baking dish, pour in enough boiling water to come halfway up sides of dishes. Bake in moderate oven about 45 minutes or until firm. Serve hot with green peppercorn sauce.

Green Peppercorn Sauce: Combine wine, juice and peppercorns in pan, bring to boil, simmer, uncovered, about 5 minutes or until mixture is reduced to about 2 tablespoons. Quickly whisk in butter pieces over low heat.

Serves 6.

- Pots can be made 3 hours ahead. Sauce best made just before serving.
- Storage: Covered, in refrigerator.
- Freeze: Not suitable.
- Microwave: Rice and spinach suitable.

MINCE AND PESTO ROLL WITH TOMATO SALSA

½ bunch (20 leaves) English spinach
500g minced lamb
1½ cups (110g) stale breadcrumbs
1 onion, finely chopped
1 egg, lightly beaten
2 tablespoons tomato paste
1 small beef stock cube
1 tablespoon tomato paste, extra

PESTO
1 cup basil leaves, firmly packed
¼ cup pine nuts
¼ cup grated parmesan cheese
2 cloves garlic, crushed
¼ cup olive oil

TOMATO SALSA
2 (about 250g) tomatoes, peeled,
  seeded
2 green shallots, chopped
1 tablespoon olive oil
2 teaspoons balsamic vinegar
¼ teaspoon sugar

Add spinach to pan of boiling water, drain immediately; rinse under cold water, pat dry with absorbent paper.

Combine mince, breadcrumbs, onion, egg, paste and crumbled stock cube in bowl; mix well.

Press mince mixture onto greased foil to a 25cm x 30cm rectangle. Place spinach leaves over mince, spread with pesto. Roll up tightly from long side using foil as a guide. Twist ends to seal foil, place in baking dish. Bake in moderately hot oven 40 minutes.

Remove foil, brush roll with extra paste, bake further 10 minutes. Stand roll 10 minutes before slicing. Serve roll with tomato salsa.

Pesto: Blend or process all ingredients until smooth.

Tomato Salsa: Combine all ingredients in bowl; cover, stand at room temperature 2 hours before serving.

Serves 6.

■ Recipe can be made a day ahead.
■ Storage: Covered, in refrigerator.
■ Freeze: Not suitable.
■ Microwave: Spinach suitable.

ONION BUNS WITH LAMB AND CHUTNEY FILLING

2 cups self-raising flour
1 large (about 200g) onion, chopped
1 tablespoon chopped fresh chives
½ cup yogurt
½ cup milk, approximately
1 egg, lightly beaten

FILLING
1 tablespoon oil
2 cloves garlic, crushed
1 teaspoon paprika
1 teaspoon ground cinnamon
250g minced lamb
2 green shallots, chopped
2 tablespoons chutney

Sift flour into large bowl, stir in onion and chives. Add yogurt and enough milk to form a soft dough. Knead on lightly floured surface until smooth. Divide dough into 12 portions. Shape each portion into a bun, place level tablespoons of filling in centre of each bun, pull dough over to cover mince. Place buns on lightly greased oven tray, brush with egg. Bake in moderately hot oven about 20 minutes or until cooked through.

Filling: Heat oil in pan, add garlic, paprika and cinnamon, cook, stirring, 1 minute. Add mince, cook, stirring, until browned. Stir in shallots and chutney; cool.

Makes 12.

- Recipe can be made a day ahead.
- Storage: Covered, in refrigerator.
- Freeze: Suitable.
- Microwave: Not suitable.

LAMB AND WATER CHESTNUTS IN LETTUCE CUPS

1 cup (30g) dried Chinese mushrooms
1 tablespoon oil
250g minced lamb
6 green shallots, chopped
200g can crab, drained
230g can sliced water chestnuts, drained, chopped
½ x 230g can bamboo shoots, drained, chopped
1 teaspoon sesame oil
1 tablespoon light soy sauce
2 teaspoons oyster sauce
2 tablespoons dry sherry
8 lettuce leaves

Place mushrooms in bowl, cover with boiling water, stand 20 minutes, drain; discard stems, chop caps finely. Heat oil in pan, add mince, stir over heat until browned. Add mushrooms, shallots, crab, chestnuts and bamboo shoots, cook, stirring, 2 minutes; stir in sesame oil, sauces and sherry; cool.

Serve mixture in lettuce leaves.

Serves 4.

- Mince can be made a day ahead.
- Storage: Covered, in refrigerator.
- Freeze: Mince mixture suitable.
- Microwave: Suitable.

CHICKEN RAVIOLI WITH PESTO

It is important to use 60g eggs in this recipe for ravioli.
2 cups plain flour
3 eggs, lightly beaten
grated fresh parmesan cheese

FILLING
350g minced chicken
1 egg yolk
½ teaspoon cracked black peppercorns

PESTO SAUCE
½ cup firmly packed basil leaves
1 clove garlic, crushed
1 tablespoon pine nuts, toasted
½ cup olive oil

Process flour and eggs until mixture forms a ball. Knead dough on lightly floured surface until smooth and elastic. Cut dough in half, roll each half through pasta machine on thickest setting. Fold dough in half, roll through machine again. Repeat rolling and folding several times until dough is very smooth and elastic; dust dough with a little extra flour when necessary. Roll dough through machine, adjust setting to become less thick with each roll; dust dough with a little extra flour when necessary. Roll to 1mm thickness (No.7 on pasta machine).

Cut dough into 10cm wide strips. Place 2 level teaspoons of filling 6cm apart over 1 strip of dough. Brush a little water lightly between fillings; top with another strip of dough; press firmly between fillings and along edges of dough. Cut into squares with pastry wheel. Sprinkle ravioli with a little extra flour. Repeat with remaining pasta and filling.

Add ravioli to large pan of boiling water just before serving. Boil, uncovered, about 5 minutes or until ravioli is just tender; drain. Serve ravioli with pesto sauce, sprinkled with parmesan cheese.

Filling: Combine all ingredients in bowl; mix well.

Pesto Sauce: Blend or process all ingredients until smooth.

Serves 4 to 6.

- Ravioli best made just before serving.
- Freeze: Uncooked ravioli suitable.
- Microwave: Suitable.

FAR LEFT: Clockwise from left: Onion Buns with Lamb and Chutney Filling, Lamb and Water Chestnuts in Lettuce Cups, Mince and Pesto Roll with Tomato Salsa.
LEFT: Chicken Ravioli with Pesto.

KUMARA PASTRIES WITH PUMPKIN DHAL

4 cups plain flour
pinch turmeric
250g butter
2 teaspoons cumin seeds
2 egg yolks
2/3 cup water, approximately
1 egg, lightly beaten

FILLING
150g kumara
1 small (about 100g) potato
1 tablespoon oil
2 cloves garlic, crushed
1/2 teaspoon ground cumin
1/2 teaspoon ground coriander
1/4 teaspoon turmeric
1/4 teaspoon garam masala
2 teaspoons paprika
400g minced beef
1 small beef stock cube
1 small green pepper, finely chopped
1/2 cup water
2 tablespoons currants

PUMPKIN DHAL
400g pumpkin, chopped
2 teaspoons oil
1 teaspoon curry powder
1/2 teaspoon paprika
2 teaspoons castor sugar
425g can garbanzos, rinsed, drained
1/2 cup sour cream
1/2 cup finely chopped dates

Sift flour and turmeric into bowl, rub in butter, stir in seeds, egg yolks and enough water to make ingredients cling together. Knead dough on floured surface until smooth, cover, refrigerate 30 minutes.

Roll pastry on lightly floured surface until 2mm thick; cut into 12cm squares. Spoon 2 level tablespoons filling onto each square, brush edges with water, fold in half to enclose filling, seal with fork. Brush pastries with egg. Make 2 slits in pastry, place on lightly greased oven trays. Bake in moderately hot oven about 20 minutes or until browned. Serve hot or cold with pumpkin dhal.

Filling: Cut kumara and potato into 1cm cubes. Heat oil in pan, add garlic, spices and mince, stir over heat until mince is well browned. Add kumara, potato, crumbled stock cube, and remaining ingredients; bring to boil, simmer, uncovered, until vegetables are tender and liquid evaporated.

Pumpkin Dhal: Boil, steam or microwave pumpkin until tender. Heat oil in pan, add spices, cook, stirring, until aromatic; stir in pumpkin, sugar and garbanzos; cool. Blend or process mixture until smooth, stir in sour cream and dates.

Makes about 20.

- Pastries can be prepared a day ahead; dhal, 3 days ahead.
- Storage: Covered, in refrigerator.
- Freeze: Uncooked pastries suitable.
- Microwave: Pumpkin suitable.

LAMB AND SHALLOT DUMPLINGS

1 cup plain flour
1 egg, lightly beaten
1 egg yolk
1 tablespoon oil
1 tablespoon water, approximately
2 tablespoons oil, extra
1/2 cup water, extra
1 tablespoon light soy sauce

FILLING
150g minced lamb
2 green shallots, chopped
1 clove garlic, crushed
2 teaspoons light soy sauce
pinch chilli powder

Sift flour into bowl, add combined egg, egg yolk and oil with enough water to form a firm dough.

Knead dough on lightly floured surface

about 4 minutes or until smooth; cover, refrigerate 30 minutes.

Roll dough on lightly floured surface until 1mm thick (No. 7 on pasta machine). Cut dough into 8cm rounds, place level teaspoons of filling on each round. Brush edges with water, fold rounds in half, pinch edges together to seal.

Heat extra oil in large pan, add dumplings in single layer. Cook until lightly browned underneath, add combined extra water and sauce, simmer, covered, about 5 minutes or until dumplings are browned underneath.
Filling: Combine all ingredients in bowl; mix well.

Makes about 24.
- Dumplings can be prepared a day ahead.
- Storage: Covered, in refrigerator.
- Freeze: Uncooked dumplings suitable.
- Microwave: Not suitable.

VINE LEAF AND LAMB ROLLS

200g packet vine leaves in brine, rinsed, drained
500g minced lamb
1 onion, finely chopped
½ cup chopped fresh mint
1 cup chopped fresh parsley
½ teaspoon dried thyme leaves
¼ cup cooked rice
2 x 375g cartons condensed vegetable stock

DRESSING
1 tablespoon olive oil
1 tablespoon lemon juice

Place leaves in bowl, cover with boiling water, stand 1 hour; drain, reserve water. Rinse leaves under cold water; drain well.

Combine mince, onion, herbs and rice in bowl, mix well. Place leaves smooth side down on board, place level tablespoons of mince mixture onto each leaf, fold sides in to form rolls.

Place rolls in a single layer in pan, pour in combined stock and enough of the reserved water to just cover rolls. Place upturned plate on top of rolls to prevent them from moving during cooking. Bring to boil, simmer, covered, about 45 minutes or until tender. Remove rolls from pan; drain; serve drizzled with dressing.
Dressing: Combine oil and juice in jar; shake well.

Makes about 30.
- Recipe can be made a day ahead.
- Storage: Covered, in refrigerator.
- Freeze: Not suitable.
- Microwave: Suitable.

LEFT: Kumara Pastries with Pumpkin Dahl.
RIGHT: From top: Vine Leaf and Lamb Rolls, Lamb and Shallot Dumplings.

MAIN COURSES

It will be temptingly easy to lift your ideas about minced meat from the ordinary to extraordinary when you're thinking about the family's dinner – and dinner parties! For a dinner party, consider seasoned rolled veal with red peppers or boned seasoned chicken with tomato salsa. Your family would enjoy them, too, as they would our mouth-watering recipes ranging through pastries, pasta, pies, patties, stir-fries, crepes, meatloaves, meatballs and many more. We've also included our best bolognaise sauce as a standby for making tasty pasta meals.

FRIED NOODLES WITH GARLIC BEEF

150g rice vermicelli
2 tablespoons oil
500g minced beef
1 tablespoon sweet chilli sauce
1 tablespoon black bean sauce
2 tablespoons dark soy sauce
3 cloves garlic, crushed
1 (about 120g) carrot, thinly sliced
100g broccoli, chopped
80g snow peas
2 tablespoons dark soy sauce, extra

Cover vermicelli with warm water in bowl, stand 10 minutes; drain well.

Heat oil in wok or pan, add mince, stir-fry until well browned. Add sweet chilli, black bean and dark soy sauces, garlic, carrot, broccoli and snow peas, stir-fry until vegetables are just tender.

Add vermicelli and extra soy sauce to wok, stir gently until heated through. Serve immediately.

Serves 4.

■ Recipe best made just before serving.
■ Freeze: Not suitable.
■ Microwave: Not suitable.

Fried Noodles with Garlic Beef.

LAMB AND BEAN CASSEROLE

3 bacon rashers, chopped
2 onions, sliced
2 cloves garlic, crushed
750g minced lamb
410g can tomatoes
2 tablespoons tomato paste
2 tablespoons chutney
2 tablespoons chopped fresh parsley
1 bay leaf
310g can butter beans, drained

Cook bacon in pan until crisp. Add onion and garlic to pan, cook, stirring, until onion is soft. Add mince, cook, stirring, until mince is browned. Stir in undrained crushed tomatoes, paste, chutney, parsley and bay leaf. Pour mixture into ovenproof dish (6 cup capacity), bake, covered, in moderately slow oven 1 hour. Stir in beans, bake further 10 minutes, or until hot.

Serves 4.

■ Recipe can be made 2 days ahead.
■ Storage: Covered, in refrigerator.
■ Freeze: Suitable.
■ Microwave: Suitable.

MEATBALLS IN LEMON CAPER SAUCE

500g minced lamb
1 clove garlic, crushed
1 onion, grated
1 egg, lightly beaten
½ cup packaged breadcrumbs
¼ cup rolled oats
plain flour
oil for deep-frying

LEMON CAPER SAUCE
40g butter
2 tablespoons plain flour
1½ cups water
¼ cup lemon juice
2 tablespoons sour cream
1 tablespoon drained capers
2 tablespoons chopped fresh parsley

Combine mince, garlic, onion, egg, breadcrumbs and oats in bowl, mix well. Roll level tablespoons of mixture into balls, toss in flour; shake away excess flour. Deep-fry meatballs in hot oil until well browned; drain on absorbent paper. Serve with warm lemon caper sauce.
Lemon Caper Sauce: Melt butter in pan, stir in flour, stir over heat until bubbling. Remove from heat, gradually stir in water and juice, stir over heat until sauce boils and thickens. Add cream, capers and parsley, stir until heated through.

Serves 4.

■ Meatballs can be made a day ahead.
■ Storage: Covered, in refrigerator.
■ Freeze: Meatballs suitable.
■ Microwave: Sauce suitable.

BAKED PEPPERS WITH CRUNCHY TOPPING

1 cup (90g) macaroni
30g butter
1 onion, chopped
250g minced lamb
410g can tomatoes
2 tablespoons tomato paste
2 small (about 130g) zucchini, chopped
3 large red peppers
6 slices bread
60g butter, extra
1½ cups (190g) grated tasty cheese

PORK AND VEAL PARCELS WITH APRICOT SAUCE

425g can apricot halves in syrup, drained
370g minced pork and veal
1 small onion, chopped
1 clove garlic, crushed
1 teaspoon grated fresh ginger
2 tablespoons chopped fresh coriander
2 tablespoons stale breadcrumbs
plain flour
2 tablespoons olive oil
16 sheets fillo pastry
100g butter, melted
½ cup stale breadcrumbs, extra

APRICOT SAUCE
1 teaspoon ground cumin
2 tablespoons mango chutney
⅓ cup apricot nectar

Finely chop 10 apricot halves. Reserve remaining apricots for sauce.

Combine chopped apricots, mince, onion, garlic, ginger, coriander and breadcrumbs in bowl; mix well. Shape mixture into 8 patties with floured hands. Cook patties in hot oil until browned; drain on absorbent paper.

Layer 4 sheets of pastry together, brushing each with butter and sprinkling with extra breadcrumbs. Divide pastry in half, place 1 patty on each half, fold into parcels, brush with remaining butter. Place on greased oven tray, bake, uncovered, in moderate oven about 25 minutes or until browned. Serve parcels with apricot sauce.

Apricot Sauce: Blend or process reserved apricots, cumin, chutney and nectar until smooth.

Serves 4.

■ Recipe can be prepared a day ahead.
■ Storage: Covered in refrigerator.
■ Freeze: Uncooked parcels suitable.
■ Microwave: Not suitable.

LEFT: Clockwise from back: Lamb and Bean Casserole, Baked Peppers with Crunchy Topping, Meatballs in Lemon Caper Sauce. BELOW: Pork and Veal Parcels with Apricot Sauce.

Left: Tablecloth, tea-towels and servers from Between the Sheets; china from Wedgwood Countryware. Below: Plate from Kenwick Galleries.

Add pasta to large pan of boiling water, boil, uncovered, until just tender, drain.

Meanwhile, heat butter in pan, add onion, cook, stirring, until soft. Add mince, stir over heat until well browned. Add undrained crushed tomatoes, paste and zucchini, bring to boil, simmer, uncovered, about 2 minutes or until slightly thickened. Cut peppers in half lengthways, remove seeds and membrane. Fill peppers with mince mixture, place on oven tray.

Remove crusts from bread, cut bread into 1cm cubes. Heat extra butter in pan, add bread, cook, stirring, until cubes are lightly browned. Combine croutons and cheese in bowl, sprinkle evenly over filled peppers. Bake peppers, uncovered, in moderate oven about 20 minutes or until cheese is melted and peppers are tender.

Serves 4 to 6.

■ Recipe best made just before serving.
■ Freeze: Not suitable.
■ Microwave: Pasta suitable.

SPINACH AND BEEF PIE WITH COCONUT CRUST

1 bunch (40 leaves) English spinach
1 cup (90g) coconut
2²/₃ cups milk
1 tablespoon oil
2 teaspoons ground cumin
2 teaspoons ground cinnamon
½ teaspoon turmeric
¼ teaspoon chilli powder
3 cloves garlic, crushed
750g minced beef
2 tablespoons lemon juice
¼ cup rice flour
40g butter, melted

Boil, steam or microwave spinach until just wilted, drain well, chop. Combine coconut and milk in pan, bring to boil, simmer, uncovered, 5 minutes; remove from heat, cool.

Heat oil in pan, add spices, cook, stirring until fragrant. Add garlic and mince, cook, stirring, until mince is well browned, stir in spinach and lemon juice. Spoon mince mixture into shallow ovenproof dish (6 cup capacity).

Drain milk from coconut, reserve milk and coconut.

Blend rice flour with reserved milk in pan, stir over heat until mixture boils and thickens. Pour over mince mixture.

Combine reserved coconut and butter in bowl, sprinkle over pie, bake, uncovered, in moderate oven about 40 minutes or until coconut is browned.

Serves 4 to 6.

- ■ Recipe can be made a day ahead.
- ■ Storage: Covered, in refrigerator.
- ■ Freeze: Not suitable.
- ■ Microwave: Spinach suitable.

CABBAGE ROLLS WITH TOMATO SAUCE

12 large cabbage leaves
¼ cup boiling water
1 small chicken stock cube

FILLING
2 tablespoons oil
1 onion, chopped
1 (about 120g) carrot, finely chopped
1 stick celery, finely chopped
250g minced pork and veal
125g mushrooms, chopped
1 cup cooked rice
1 teaspoon grated lemon rind
1 tablespoon light soy sauce

TOMATO SAUCE
400g can tomatoes
¼ cup dry red wine
½ teaspoon sugar
1 clove garlic, crushed
1 teaspoon chicken stock powder

Remove thick stalks from cabbage leaves; add leaves to large pan of boiling water, simmer, uncovered, until leaves are soft. Rinse leaves under cold water, drain well.

MEATBALLS IN TOMATO SAUCE

1kg minced beef
2 onions, finely chopped
2 cloves garlic, crushed
2 tablespoons chopped fresh parsley
1 tablespoon chopped fresh coriander
1 teaspoon ground cumin
1 teaspoon ground cinnamon
½ teaspoon ground ginger

TOMATO SAUCE
2 tablespoons oil
3 large (about 750g) tomatoes, peeled, chopped
2 tablespoons tomato paste
2 small fresh red chillies, chopped
1 tablespoon chopped fresh parsley
½ teaspoon ground cumin
½ teaspoon ground cinnamon
pinch cayenne pepper

Combine all ingredients in bowl; mix well. Roll level tablespoons of mixture into balls. Add meatballs to tomato sauce, bring to boil, simmer, covered, about 1 hour or until meatballs are cooked and sauce thickened. Serve with pasta, sprinkled with chopped parsley, if desired.
Tomato Sauce: Heat oil in pan, add tomatoes, cook, stirring, 10 minutes, add remaining ingredients, stir over heat until well combined.

Serves 6.

- ■ Recipe can be made a day ahead.
- ■ Storage: Covered, in refrigerator.
- ■ Freeze: Suitable.
- ■ Microwave: Not suitable.

Place ¼ cup filling in centre of each leaf; roll up to enclose filling. Place rolls close together, seam side down, in greased shallow ovenproof dish; pour over combined water and crumbled stock cube. Bake, covered, in moderate oven about 40 minutes or until heated through. Serve with tomato sauce.

Filling: Heat oil in pan, add onion, carrot and celery, cook, stirring, until vegetables are almost tender. Stir in mince, cook, stirring, until well browned. Stir in mushrooms, cook, stirring, 2 minutes. Stir in rice, rind and sauce; mix well.

Tomato Sauce: Combine undrained crushed tomatoes with remaining ingredients in pan, stir over heat, simmer, uncovered, until slightly thickened.

Serves 4.

■ Recipe can be made a day ahead.
■ Storage: Covered, in refrigerator.
■ Freeze: Not suitable.
■ Microwave: Suitable.

SPICY NOODLES WITH PORK AND CASHEWS

375g packet fresh egg noodles
2 tablespoons oil
1 teaspoon grated fresh ginger
1 clove garlic, crushed
1 teaspoon sambal oelek
500g minced pork and veal
2 tablespoons hoi sin sauce
½ teaspoon sesame oil
1 small chicken stock cube
1 cup water
2 teaspoons cornflour
2 tablespoons light soy sauce
2 tablespoons chopped fresh coriander
1 cup (150g) roasted unsalted cashews

Add noodles to large pan of boiling water, simmer, uncovered, about 3 minutes or until noodles are just tender; drain.

Heat oil in pan, add ginger, garlic, sambal oelek and mince, cook, stirring, until mince is browned. Stir in hoi sin sauce, sesame oil, crumbled stock cube, water and blended cornflour and soy sauce, stir over heat until mixture boils and thickens. Stir in noodles, coriander and cashews; stir over heat until hot.

Serves 4.

■ Recipe best made just before serving.
■ Freeze: Not suitable.
■ Microwave: Noodles suitable.

ABOVE LEFT: From back: Spinach and Beef Pie with Coconut Crust, Meatballs in Tomato Sauce.
RIGHT: From top: Spicy Noodles with Pork and Cashews, Cabbage Rolls with Tomato Sauce.

Right: China from Wedgwood.

STEAK TARTARE

You will need the best quality beef, freshly minced, for this recipe.

8 slices white bread
30g butter, melted
600g minced beef eye fillet
4 egg yolks

DRESSING
½ cup olive oil
¼ teaspoon tabasco sauce
½ teaspoon Worcestershire sauce
1 tablespoon brandy
⅔ cup lemon juice
1 teaspoon cracked black
   peppercorns
⅓ cup chopped drained capers
4 green shallots, chopped
⅓ cup chopped fresh parsley
8 anchovy fillets, chopped

Remove crusts from bread; cut in half diagonally. Brush bread with butter, place on oven trays, bake in moderately hot oven about 15 minutes or until lightly browned and crisp, turning once.

Divide mince into 4 portions on serving plates, top each portion with an egg yolk.

Serve each portion with dressing and toast. Stir in egg yolk and enough dressing to taste.

Dressing: Combine all ingredients in bowl; mix well.

Serves 4.

- Toasts can be made a day ahead. Recipe best made just before serving.
- Storage: Toasts, airtight container.
- Freeze: Not suitable.
- Microwave: Not suitable.

CHEESY BEEF PEPPERS

4 small green peppers
1 tablespoon oil
1 onion, chopped
2 cloves garlic, crushed
250g minced beef
400g can tomatoes
1 teaspoon sugar
2 tablespoons tomato paste
½ teaspoon dried sage leaves
1 cup cooked rice
200g mozzarella cheese, chopped

Slice off stem end of peppers. Discard stem ends. Carefully remove seeds and membrane in peppers. Add peppers to large pan of boiling water, simmer, uncovered, 2 minutes; rinse under cold water; drain well.

Heat oil in pan, add onion, garlic and mince, cook, stirring, until mince is well browned. Stir in undrained crushed tomatoes, sugar and paste. Bring to boil, simmer, uncovered, about 10 minutes or until liquid is evaporated and mixture thickened. Stir in sage and rice; cool, stir in cheese.

Fill peppers with mince mixture, place in greased shallow ovenproof dish. Cover peppers, bake in moderate oven about 40 minutes or until peppers are tender.

Serves 2 to 4.

- Peppers can be prepared a day ahead.
- Storage: Covered, in refrigerator.
- Freeze: Not suitable.
- Microwave: Suitable.

BEST BOLOGNAISE SAUCE

1 tablespoon olive oil
2 onions, chopped
1 clove garlic, crushed
1kg minced beef
2 x 410g cans tomatoes
1½ cups water
½ cup dry white wine
2 tablespoons tomato paste
3 teaspoons beef stock powder
1 teaspoon dried oregano leaves
½ teaspoon dried marjoram leaves
½ teaspoon sugar

Heat oil in pan, add onions and garlic, cook, stirring, over low heat about 15 minutes or until onions are soft. Add mince, cook, stirring, until well browned. Stir in remaining ingredients. Bring to boil, simmer, uncovered, about 2 hours or until sauce is thickened, stirring occasionally. Serve with pasta, if desired.

Serves 4.

- Sauce can be made 2 days ahead.
- Storage: Covered, in refrigerator.
- Freeze: Suitable.
- Microwave: Not suitable.

BLUE CHEESE MEATLOAF

2 bacon rashers, chopped
100g mushrooms, chopped
350g minced beef
1 small beef stock cube
1 small onion, grated
½ teaspoon dried oregano leaves
½ teaspoon dried thyme leaves
2 tablespoons tomato paste
100g light blue cheese, chopped
1 egg, lightly beaten
1 egg white
1½ cups (110g) stale breadcrumbs
75g double smoked ham, chopped

TOPPING
50g light blue cheese, softened
1 tablespoon sour light cream
75g double smoked ham, finely
 chopped
pinch chilli powder
2 tablespoons stale breadcrumbs

Cook bacon in hot pan until lightly browned, add mushrooms, cook, stirring, until mushrooms are soft; drain.

Process mince, crumbled stock cube, onion, herbs, paste, cheese, egg, egg white and breadcrumbs until combined and pasty. Transfer mixture to bowl, mix in bacon mixture and ham. Press mixture into greased 8cm x 26cm bar pan. Bake, uncovered, in moderate oven about 45 minutes or until cooked through. Stand 5 minutes, drain away excess liquid; turn onto oven tray.

Spread topping over meatloaf. Bake, uncovered, in hot oven 10 minutes or until heated through.

Topping: Combine all ingredients in bowl, mix well.

Serves 4.

■ Recipe can be prepared a day ahead.
■ Storage: Covered, in refrigerator.
■ Freeze: Meatloaf without topping suitable.
■ Microwave: Not suitable.

LEFT: Steak Tartare.
ABOVE: Clockwise from top: Best Bolognaise Sauce, Cheesy Beef Peppers, Blue Cheese Meatloaf.

LAMB, APRICOT AND CHICK PEA CURRY

1 cup (190g) dried chick peas
1 tablespoon olive oil
¼ teaspoon chilli powder
½ teaspoon turmeric
½ teaspoon ground coriander
½ teaspoon ground cumin
¼ teaspoon garam masala
1 clove garlic, crushed
3 onions, chopped
750g minced lamb
1 tablespoon plain flour
2 sticks celery, chopped
400g can tomatoes
2 cups water
2 teaspoons sugar
⅔ cup dried apricots, halved

Cover chick peas with hot water in bowl, cover, stand overnight; drain.

Heat oil in pan, add spices, garlic, onions and mince, cook, stirring, until mince is well browned. Stir in flour, cook, stirring, 2 minutes. Remove from heat, stir in chick peas, celery, undrained crushed tomatoes, water and sugar, stir over heat until mixture boils and thickens. Simmer, covered, 30 minutes, add apricots, simmer, uncovered, about 15 minutes or until chick peas are tender and mixture thickened slightly. Serve curry with rice, cherry tomatoes and onions, if desired.

Serves 6.

■ Recipe can be made a day ahead.
■ Storage: Covered, in refrigerator.
■ Freeze: Suitable.
■ Microwave: Not suitable.

LAMB PATTIES WITH TOMATO AND MOZZARELLA

500g minced lamb
1 egg, lightly beaten
1 onion, chopped
2 tablespoons chutney
1 tablespoon chopped fresh parsley
¼ teaspoon cracked black peppercorns
2 tablespoons oil
1 large (about 250g) tomato, sliced
1 tablespoon chopped fresh basil
2 cups (200g) grated mozzarella cheese

Combine mince, egg, onion, chutney, parsley and peppercorns in bowl; mix well. Shape mixture into 6 patties. Cook patties in hot oil until browned; drain on absorbent paper.

Transfer patties to oven tray, top with tomato, basil and cheese, grill until cheese is melted and browned.

Serves 4 to 6.

■ Patties can be prepared a day ahead.
■ Storage: Covered, in refrigerator.
■ Freeze: Uncooked patties suitable.
■ Microwave: Not suitable.

PASTA BOWS WITH PORK AND BASIL PUREE

1 tablespoon olive oil
1 small onion, chopped
3 cloves garlic, crushed
500g minced pork and veal
200g mushrooms, chopped
1 cup dry white wine
1 teaspoon chicken stock powder
½ cup water
500g pasta bows

BASIL PUREE
1 cup fresh basil leaves, firmly packed
1 cup fresh parsley sprigs, firmly packed
¼ cup pine nuts, toasted
¼ cup olive oil

Heat oil in pan, add onion and garlic, cook, stirring, until onion is soft. Add mince, stir over heat until mince is well browned. Stir in mushrooms, wine, stock powder and water, bring to boil, simmer, uncovered, 15 minutes. Process mince mixture until coarsely chopped, stir in basil puree.

Meanwhile, add pasta to large pan of boiling water, boil, uncovered, until just tender; drain. Serve mince over pasta.
Basil Puree: Blend or process all ingredients until well combined.

Serves 4.

■ Recipe best made just before serving.
■ Freeze: Not suitable.
■ Microwave: Pasta suitable.

PORK AND VEAL CASSEROLE WITH POLENTA TOPPING

1 tablespoon oil
2 onions, chopped
500g minced pork and veal
1 green pepper, chopped
¼ cup tomato paste
410g can tomatoes
2 teaspoons ground cumin
1 teaspoon chilli powder
1 tablespoon Worcestershire sauce
440g can corn kernels, drained
1 tablespoon polenta
½ cup water
1 cup (125g) grated tasty cheese

TOPPING
1½ cups self raising flour
1 cup (200g) polenta
60g butter
1 cup milk

Heat oil in pan, add onions and mince, cook, stirring, until mince is well browned. Stir in pepper, paste, undrained crushed tomatoes, cumin, chilli powder, sauce, corn, polenta and water. Bring to boil, simmer, uncovered, about 10 minutes or until thickened. Pour mince mixture into greased ovenproof dish (6 cup capacity). Drop tablespoons of topping onto mince mixture; sprinkle with cheese. Bake, uncovered, in hot oven 10 minutes, reduce heat to moderate, bake about 30 minutes or until topping is cooked.
Topping: Sift flour into medium bowl, stir in polenta, rub in butter, stir in milk.

Serves 6.

■ Mince can be made a day ahead.
■ Storage: Covered, in refrigerator.
■ Freeze: Suitable.
■ Microwave: Not suitable.

LEFT: From left: Lamb, Apricot and Chick Pea Curry, Lamb Patties with Tomato and Mozzarella.
ABOVE: From top: Pasta Bows with Pork and Basil Puree, Pork and Veal Casserole with Polenta Topping.

LEFT: Fabric and candlestick from Between the Sheets; serving ware from Mandura Imports.

Reserve 2 tablespoons pan juices, cover lamb with foil.

Heat pan juices in pan, add flour, stir over heat until flour is lightly browned. Remove from heat, gradually stir in combined water and stock powder. Stir over heat until sauce boils and thickens; strain. Serve lamb with sauce and meatballs.

Serves 4 to 6.

- ▥ Recipe can be prepared 3 hours ahead.
- ▥ Storage: Covered, in refrigerator.
- ▥ Freeze: Seasoned lamb and meatballs suitable.
- ▥ Microwave: Not suitable.

SPICED BEEF PASTA SALAD

**1 tablespoon oil
500g minced beef
1 teaspoon ground coriander
1 teaspoon ground cumin
¼ teaspoon chilli powder
½ teaspoon paprika
1 red pepper
1 yellow pepper
150g green beans, chopped
250g penne pasta
2 teaspoons chopped fresh coriander**

DRESSING
**2 tablespoons light soy sauce
¼ cup dry sherry
1 tablespoon mirin
1 tablespoon honey
2 tablespoons tomato sauce**

Heat oil in pan, add mince and spices, cook, stirring, until mince is browned; remove from heat, cool.

Quarter peppers, remove seeds and membrane. Grill peppers, skin side up, until skin blisters and blackens. Remove skin from peppers, cut peppers into strips.

Boil, steam or microwave beans until just tender, rinse under cold water; drain. Combine mince mixture, peppers and beans in bowl; cover, refrigerate 1 hour.

Add pasta to large pan of boiling water, boil, uncovered, until just tender; drain. Combine mince mixture, pasta, coriander and dressing in bowl; mix well.

Dressing: Combine all ingredients in jar; shake well.

Serves 4.

- ▥ Salad can be made 3 hours ahead.
- ▥ Storage: Covered, in refrigerator.
- ▥ Freeze: Not suitable.
- ▥ Microwave: Pasta and beans suitable.

ROAST SEASONED LAMB WITH SAGE MEATBALLS

**1 tablespoon oil
60g butter
1 large (about 200g) onion, chopped
1 clove garlic, crushed
100g mushrooms, chopped
4 bacon rashers, chopped
1 tablespoon chopped fresh sage
500g minced lamb
1 egg, lightly beaten
oil for deep-frying
1½kg shoulder lamb, boned
1½ tablespoons plain flour
1½ cups water
1 teaspoon chicken stock powder**

Heat oil and butter in pan, add onion, garlic, mushrooms and bacon, cook, stirring until onion is soft; cool. Combine onion mixture, sage and mince in bowl; mix well.

Divide mixture in half. Reserve half for seasoning; add egg to remaining mixture; mix well. Roll level tablespoons of remaining mixture into balls with floured hands. Deep-fry meatballs in hot oil in batches until browned and cooked through; drain on absorbent paper.

Open lamb out on bench, spoon reserved mince seasoning along centre. Roll lamb to enclose seasoning, secure with string at 3cm intervals, place in baking dish. Bake, uncovered, in moderate oven about 1 hour or until lamb is tender.

Remove lamb from baking dish.

ABOVE LEFT: Roast Seasoned Lamb with Sage Meatballs.

Tea-towel from Between the Sheets; china from Wedgwood Spode.

BEEF AND PUMPKIN SLICE

750g minced beef
2 eggs, lightly beaten
1 onion, finely chopped
⅓ cup chutney
1 tablespoon chopped fresh thyme
⅓ cup tomato sauce

PUMPKIN FILLING
1kg pumpkin, chopped
20g butter
1 onion, chopped
2 eggs, lightly beaten

Line 26cm x 32cm Swiss roll pan with foil.
Combine mince, eggs, onion, chutney and thyme in bowl; mix well. Spread base of prepared pan evenly with half the mince mixture, top with pumpkin filling. Press remaining mince mixture onto a sheet of foil large enough to fit pan, place over filling, remove foil. Brush slice with sauce, bake, uncovered, in moderate oven about 1 hour or until firm. Stand slice 5 minutes before cutting.
Filling: Boil, steam or microwave pumpkin until just tender; drain, cool. Mash pumpkin until smooth. Heat butter in pan, add onion, cook, stirring, until soft.

Combine pumpkin, onion and eggs in bowl; mix well.

Serves 4 to 6.

▪ Recipe can be made a day ahead.
▪ Storage: Covered, in refrigerator.
▪ Freeze: Suitable.
▪ Microwave: Pumpkin suitable.

BELOW: From top: Spiced Beef Pasta Salad, Beef and Pumpkin Slice.

Plates from Villa Italiana; tiles from Country Floors.

MEATLOAF WITH FRUITY FILLING

400g minced beef
250g sausage mince
1 onion, grated
1 cup (70g) stale breadcrumbs
2 tablespoons chutney
1 egg, lightly beaten

FRUITY FILLING
1 cup (70g) stale breadcrumbs
1 stick celery, chopped
2 green shallots, chopped
1 tablespoon chopped fresh parsley
¼ cup chopped dried apricots
¼ cup chopped dried dates
1 teaspoon grated orange rind
2 tablespoons orange juice
½ teaspoon garam masala
1 egg, lightly beaten

HERBED MAYONNAISE
1 cup mayonnaise
2 teaspoons seeded mustard
2 teaspoons chopped fresh mint

Combine minces, onion, breadcrumbs, chutney and egg in bowl; mix well. Press two-thirds of mixture over base and sides of lightly greased ovenproof dish (6 cup capacity); press fruity filling into centre, cover with remaining mixture. Cover, bake in moderate oven about 1 hour or until cooked through. Drain away excess juices, stand 5 minutes before cutting.
Fruity Filling: Combine all ingredients in bowl; mix well.
Herbed Mayonnaise: Combine all ingredients in bowl; mix well.

Serves 6.

■ Recipe can be made a day ahead.
■ Storage: Covered, in refrigerator.
■ Freeze: Not suitable.
■ Microwave: Suitable.

SPICY COCONUT MINCE

2 tablespoons oil
1 onion, chopped
2 cloves garlic, crushed
750g minced beef
2 teaspoons grated fresh ginger
1 teaspoon sambal oelek
2 teaspoons ground coriander
2 teaspoons ground cumin
1 cup water
1 small beef stock cube
¼ cup tomato puree
400ml can coconut milk
1 tablespoon chopped fresh
**   coriander**
2 cups long grain rice
pinch ground saffron

Heat oil in pan, add onion and garlic, cook, stirring, until onion is soft. Add mince, cook, stirring, until mince is well browned. Stir in ginger, sambal oelek, coriander and cumin; cook, stirring, 1 minute.
Stir in water, crumbled stock cube and puree, bring to boil, simmer, covered, 5 minutes. Stir in coconut milk and

coriander, stir until heated through.
Divide rice between 2 pans of boiling water, add saffron to 1 pan, boil both pans, uncovered, until rice is just tender; drain. Toss rice together, serve mince with rice.

Serves 4 to 6.

■ Casserole can be made a day ahead.
■ Storage: Covered, in refrigerator.
■ Freeze: Not suitable.
■ Microwave: Rice suitable.

PASTA WITH BEEF AND PEPPERS

500g penne pasta
1 tablespoon oil
1 onion, chopped
2 cloves garlic, crushed
500g minced beef
½ teaspoon ground fennel
410g can tomatoes
390g can pimientos, drained, sliced
½ cup water
1 small beef stock cube
1 teaspoon sugar
2 tablespoons red wine vinegar
2 tablespoons tomato paste
2 (about 200g) zucchini, thinly sliced
1 tablespoon chopped fresh chives

Add pasta to large pan of boiling water, boil, uncovered, until just tender; drain.
Heat oil in pan, add onion, garlic, mince and fennel, cook, stirring, until mince is browned. Add undrained, crushed tomatoes, pimientos, water, crumbled stock cube, sugar, vinegar and paste. Bring to boil, simmer, uncovered, 10 minutes. Add zucchini and chives, simmer, uncovered, further 10 minutes. Serve sauce with pasta.

Serves 4.

■ Recipe can be prepared a day ahead.
■ Storage: Covered, in refrigerator.
■ Freeze: Sauce suitable.
■ Microwave: Suitable.

LEFT: Clockwise from left: Pasta with Beef and Peppers, Spicy Coconut Mince, Meatloaf with Fruity Filling.

China from Villeroy & Boch.

SHEPHERD'S PIE POTS

1 tablespoon oil
1 onion, chopped
1 clove garlic, crushed
300g minced beef
150g mushrooms, chopped
410g can tomatoes
1 tablespoon Worcestershire sauce
1 teaspoon chopped fresh chives
1 teaspoon chopped fresh parsley
1 teaspoon chopped fresh sage
1 teaspoon chopped fresh rosemary
1 small beef stock cube
1 cup water

TOPPING
4 large (about 800g) potatoes,
    chopped
½ cup cream
20g butter

Heat oil in pan, add onion and garlic, cook, stirring, until onion is soft. Add mince and mushrooms, cook, stirring, until mince is browned. Stir in undrained crushed tomatoes, sauce, herbs, crumbled stock cube and water. Bring to boil, simmer, covered, 1 hour; stirring occasionally. Pour mixture into 4 ovenproof dishes (1 cup capacity). Spoon over topping, place dishes on oven tray. Bake uncovered in moderately hot oven about 20 minutes or until lightly browned.
Topping: Boil, steam or microwave potatoes until tender, drain. Mash potatoes in bowl with cream and butter.

Serves 4.

- Recipe can be prepared a day ahead.
- Storage: Covered, in refrigerator.
- Freeze: Not suitable.
- Microwave: Potatoes suitable.

CHUNKY VEGETABLE MEATLOAF

250g pumpkin, chopped
250g green beans
1 cup (70g) stale breadcrumbs
1kg sausage mince
1 egg, lightly beaten
⅓ cup chopped fresh chives
½ teaspoon dried thyme leaves
¼ cup water
¾ cup corn kernels

Boil, steam or microwave pumpkin and beans separately until just tender, drain, rinse under cold water; drain well.

Reserve 1 tablespoon breadcrumbs for topping. Combine remaining breadcrumbs, mince, egg, herbs and water in bowl; mix well. Press quarter of mince mixture over base of greased 14cm x 21cm loaf pan. Top with corn, leaving 1cm border around edge. Top with another

quarter of mince, then a layer of pumpkin. Repeat layering with remaining mince and beans, finishing with mince layer. Sprinkle with reserved breadcrumbs, slash top of loaf with knife. Bake, uncovered, in moderate oven about 1 hour. Turn meatloaf from pan; drain on absorbent paper. Stand meatloaf 10 minutes before serving.

Serves 6 to 8.

▨ Meatloaf can be made a day ahead.
▨ Storage: Covered, in refrigerator.
▨ Freeze: Not suitable.
▨ Microwave: Suitable.

PRUNE AND APPLE ROLL

1kg minced beef
1 onion, finely chopped
1 cup (70g) stale breadcrumbs
1 tablespoon chopped fresh sage
2 teaspoons chopped fresh rosemary
1 egg, lightly beaten
½ cup pitted prunes, halved
½ apple, finely chopped

APPLE SAUCE
40g butter
1 onion, finely sliced
1 tablespoon plain flour
1¼ cups apple juice
1 small chicken stock cube
2 teaspoons sugar
½ apple, thinly sliced

Combine mince, onion, breadcrumbs, herbs and egg in bowl; mix well. Spread mixture onto a piece of greased foil to form a 25cm x 35cm rectangle.

Place prunes and apple along 1 long side of mince. Roll up like a Swiss roll, using foil to lift and guide roll. Wrap foil around roll, twist ends of foil to tighten roll into shape. Place roll in a baking dish, bake in moderate oven 30 minutes, remove foil, bake further 30 minutes or until roll is tender. Stand 5 minutes before serving with apple sauce.

Apple Sauce: Heat butter in pan, add onion, cook, stirring, until soft. Stir in flour, cook, stirring, until mixture is dry and grainy. Remove from heat, gradually stir in juice, crumbled stock cube, sugar and apple. Stir over heat until mixture boils and thickens.

Serves 6.

▨ Recipe can be made a day ahead.
▨ Storage: Covered, in refrigerator.
▨ Freeze: Uncooked roll suitable.
▨ Microwave: Sauce suitable.

LEFT: From top: Chunky Vegetable Meatloaf, Shepherd's Pie Pots.

ABOVE RIGHT: From top: Rice and Mince Cake, Prune and Apple Roll.

Above right: Plates and bowl from Accoutrement.

RICE AND MINCE CAKE

2 cups cooked white rice
½ cup grated tasty cheese
¼ cup chopped fresh parsley
2 eggs, lightly beaten
¼ cup grated tasty cheese, extra

FILLING
250g packet frozen spinach, thawed
30g butter
1 onion, chopped
2 cloves garlic, crushed
500g minced beef
1 cup (70g) stale breadcrumbs
3 hard-boiled eggs, chopped

Lightly grease 23cm springform tin, cover base with paper, grease paper.

Combine rice, cheese, parsley and eggs in bowl. Press half of rice mixture over base of prepared tin, top with filling. Press remaining rice mixture over mince. Bake, uncovered, in moderate oven about 1 hour or until cooked through. Sprinkle with extra cheese, bake further 10 minutes or until cheese is melted. Stand 5 minutes before removing from tin.

Filling: Squeeze spinach to remove liquid. Heat butter in pan, add onion and garlic, cook, stirring, until onion is soft. Combine spinach, onion mixture, mince and breadcrumbs in bowl, stir in hard-boiled eggs; mix well.

Serves 6.

▨ Recipe can be made a day ahead.
▨ Storage: Covered, in refrigerator.
▨ Freeze: Not suitable.
▨ Microwave: Not suitable.

CHEESY PUFFED RINGS WITH SPICED LAMB FILLING

70g butter
1 cup water
1 cup plain flour
4 eggs
2 cups (200g) grated jarlsberg cheese

SPICED LAMB FILLING
1 tablespoon oil
1 onion, chopped
2 cloves garlic, crushed
500g minced lamb
1 tablespoon grated fresh ginger
2 teaspoons ground coriander
2 teaspoons ground cumin
1 teaspoon garam masala
¼ teaspoon chilli powder
2 tablespoons tomato paste
2 small beef stock cubes
½ cup water

Combine butter and water in pan, bring to boil, stirring until butter is melted. Add sifted flour all at once, stir vigorously over heat until mixture leaves side of pan and forms a smooth ball.

Transfer mixture to small bowl of electric mixer (or processor). Add eggs 1 at a time, beat until smooth after each addition; stir in cheese.

Mark 4 x 12cm circles on lightly greased oven trays. Spoon mixture into piping bag without tube, pipe thickly around edges of marked circles. Bake in hot oven 12 minutes, reduce heat to moderate, bake further 12 minutes or until browned and crisp. Split puffed rings in half, return to oven for 3 minutes to dry insides completely. Spoon spiced lamb filling into base of puffed rings, replace tops. Serve hot.

Spiced Lamb Filling: Heat oil in pan, add onion, garlic and mince, cook, stirring, until onion is soft and mince browned. Add ginger and spices, cook, stirring, about 1 minute or until spices are fragrant. Stir in paste, crumbled stock cubes and water, bring to boil, simmer, uncovered, about 3 minutes or until thickened slightly.

Serves 4.

■ Recipe can be made a day ahead.
■ Storage: Puffed rings in airtight container. Filling covered, in refrigerator.
■ Freeze: Filling and rings suitable, separately.
■ Microwave: Not suitable.

BEEF MINCE WITH CHICK PEAS

1 teaspoon oil
2 cloves garlic, crushed
1 onion, chopped
500g minced beef
410g can tomatoes
2 tablespoons tomato paste
1 small beef stock cube
1 teaspoon ground allspice
310g can chick peas, rinsed, drained
100g snow peas
1 tablespoon chopped fresh parsley

Heat oil in pan, add garlic and onion, cook, stirring, until onion is soft. Add mince, cook, stirring, until mince is browned. Add undrained crushed tomatoes, paste, crumbled stock cube and allspice. Bring to boil, simmer, covered, until mince is cooked. Stir in chick peas and peas, simmer, uncovered, 5 minutes; stir in parsley.

Serves 4.

■ Recipe can be made a day ahead.
■ Storage: Covered, in refrigerator.
■ Freeze: Not suitable.
■ Microwave: Suitable.

VEGETABLE MINCE SLICE

8 thick slices bread, toasted
1 tablespoon oil
2 onions, chopped
2 cloves garlic, crushed
600g minced beef
2 tablespoons tomato paste
2 tablespoons plain flour
2 cups water
1 teaspoon dried oregano leaves
1 (about 120g) carrot, sliced
1 (about 100g) zucchini, sliced
150g mushrooms, sliced
1 red pepper, chopped
100g broccoli, chopped
2 eggs, lightly beaten
2 cups (250g) grated tasty cheese

Cut crusts from toast, cover base of greased 20cm x 30cm lamington pan with toast. Heat oil in pan, add onions and garlic, cook, stirring, until onions are soft. Add mince, stir over heat until browned, stir in paste and flour, then water and oregano. Bring to boil, simmer, covered, 20 minutes. Add vegetables, simmer, uncovered, until carrots are tender and liquid evaporated; drain mince mixture; cool.

Stir eggs into mince mixture, press over toast, sprinkle with cheese. Bake, uncovered, in moderate oven about 30 minutes or until firm.

Serves 4.

■ Mince mixture can be prepared a day ahead.
■ Storage: Covered, in refrigerator.
■ Freeze: Suitable.
■ Microwave: Not suitable.

LEFT: Cheesy Puffed Rings with Spiced Lamb Filling.
ABOVE: From top: Beef Mince with Chick Peas, Vegetable Mince Slice.

Above: Plates from Villeroy & Boch.

BOBOTIE

20g butter
2 onions, chopped
1 apple, peeled, chopped
2 teaspoons curry powder
500g minced beef
¾ cup stale breadcrumbs
1 egg
1 tablespoon mango chutney
1 tablespoon flaked almonds
1 tablespoon sultanas
4 bay leaves
¾ cup milk
1 egg, extra

Heat butter in pan, add onions and apple, cook, stirring, until onions are soft. Add curry powder, cook, stirring, further 1 minute; remove from heat, cool.

Combine curry mixture, mince, breadcrumbs, egg, chutney, almonds and sultanas in bowl; mix well. Spread mixture into greased ovenproof dish (6 cup capacity), top with bay leaves, bake, uncovered, in moderate oven 30 minutes. Whisk milk and extra egg in jug, pour over mince mixture, stir through with fork. Bake further 30 minutes, or until browned.

Serves 4.

- ▓ Recipe can be made a day ahead.
- ▓ Storage: Covered, in refrigerator.
- ▓ Freeze: Not suitable.
- ▓ Microwave: Not suitable.

PEPPERONI AND MINCE RING

750g minced beef
1 small onion, grated
1 small green pepper, finely chopped
60g sliced pepperoni, chopped
2 tablespoons tomato paste
1 egg, lightly beaten
½ cup stale breadcrumbs
⅓ cup black olives, chopped
½ teaspoon dried oregano leaves
1 cup (100g) grated mozzarella
  cheese
¼ teaspoon dried oregano leaves,
  extra

Combine mince, onion, pepper, pepperoni, paste, egg, breadcrumbs, olives and oregano in bowl; mix well. Press mixture into lightly greased 24cm savarin pan. Bake, uncovered, in moderate oven about 40 minutes. Turn loaf onto wire rack, place on flameproof tray. Sprinkle loaf with cheese and extra oregano, grill until cheese is lightly browned.

Serves 4 to 6.

- ▓ Recipe can be made a day ahead.
- ▓ Storage: Covered, in refrigerator.
- ▓ Freeze: Suitable.
- ▓ Microwave: Not suitable.

Clockwise from back right: Bobotie, Pepperoni and Mince Ring, Beef Ravioli with Creamy Tomato Sauce.

BEEF RAVIOLI WITH CREAMY TOMATO SAUCE

2 cups plain flour
¼ cup chopped fresh chives
3 eggs

FILLING
30g butter
1 onion, chopped
1 (about 120g) carrot, chopped
2 teaspoons chopped fresh thyme
500g minced beef
6 slices mortadella, chopped
⅓ cup dry red wine
1 tablespoon tomato paste
1 egg

CREAMY TOMATO SAUCE
30g butter
1 small onion, finely chopped
½ cup dry white wine
300ml carton cream
1 small beef stock cube
1 teaspoon cornflour
½ cup milk
1 tomato, peeled, seeded, chopped

Sift flour into bowl, stir in chives, make well in centre, add eggs. Using fingers, gradually mix flour into eggs. Press mixture into ball; knead dough about 5 minutes or until smooth and elastic (or process all ingredients until mixture forms a ball). Cover dough, stand 20 minutes.

Divide dough in half. Roll each half on lightly floured surface to 1mm thick. Place 2 level teaspoons of filling at 3cm intervals over dough. Brush lightly between filling with water. Top with remaining sheet of pasta, press firmly between filling and along edges. Cut into ravioli shapes using pasta wheel.

Add ravioli to large pan of boiling water, boil, uncovered, about 5 minutes or until tender; drain. Combine ravioli with creamy tomato sauce.

Filling: Heat butter in pan, add onion, carrot and thyme, cook, stirring, until onion is soft. Add mince and mortadella, cook, stirring, until mince is well browned. Add wine and paste, simmer, covered, about 5 minutes or until liquid is evaporated; cool. Process mince mixture and egg until finely chopped.

Creamy Tomato Sauce: Heat butter in pan, add onion, cook, stirring, until soft. Add wine, cook, stirring, until mixture is reduced by half. Add cream, crumbled stock cube and blended cornflour and milk. Stir over heat until mixture boils and thickens; stir in tomato.

Serves 6.

- ▓ Ravioli can be made a day ahead.
- ▓ Storage: Covered, in refrigerator.
- ▓ Freeze: Ravioli suitable.
- ▓ Microwave: Suitable.

SAVOURY CREPE STACK

¾ cup plain flour
1 cup milk
2 eggs, lightly beaten
¼ cup finely chopped chives
1 tablespoon oil
1 onion, chopped
1 clove garlic, crushed
1 red pepper, finely chopped
500g minced beef
100g mushrooms, sliced
¼ cup tomato paste
½ cup water
1 teaspoon dried oregano leaves
½ teaspoon sambal oelek
1 egg, lightly beaten, extra
½ cup grated mozzarella cheese
½ cup grated parmesan cheese

Sift flour into bowl, gradually stir in combined milk and eggs, beat until smooth, stir in chives. Cover, stand 30 minutes. Pour 2 to 3 tablespoons of batter into heated greased heavy-based pan; cook until lightly browned underneath. Turn crepe, brown other side. Repeat with remaining batter. You will need 8 crepes for this recipe.

Heat oil in pan, add onion and garlic, cook, stirring, until onion is soft. Add pepper and mince, cook, stirring, until mince changes colour. Add mushrooms, paste, water, oregano and sambal oelek. Bring to boil, simmer, covered, 20 minutes. Simmer, uncovered, further 10 minutes or until most of the liquid is evaporated; cool. Stir extra egg into mince mixture.

Place 1 crepe in greased 20cm springform tin, top with some mince mixture. Repeat layering with remaining crepes and mince, finishing with a crepe; sprinkle with combined cheeses. Stand tin on oven tray, bake, uncovered, in moderate oven about 20 minutes or until hot. Grill until cheese is lightly browned.

Serves 4.

■ Mince mixture and crepes can be prepared a day ahead.
■ Storage: Covered, in refrigerator.
■ Freeze: Crepes and mince suitable.
■ Microwave: Not suitable.

BONED SEASONED CHICKEN WITH TOMATO SALSA

2 bacon rashers, chopped
200g minced pork and veal
¼ cup stale breadcrumbs
2 tablespoons pistachios
¼ red pepper, chopped
1 teaspoon chopped fresh thyme
1 tablespoon chopped fresh parsley
1 teaspoon chicken stock powder
1.7kg chicken

TOMATO SALSA
3 (about 400g) tomatoes, chopped
1 small red Spanish onion, chopped
1 clove garlic, crushed
1 tablespoon red wine vinegar
2 tablespoons castor sugar
2 teaspoons chopped fresh thyme

Cook bacon in pan until crisp; drain on absorbent paper. Combine bacon, mince, breadcrumbs, pistachios, pepper, herbs and stock powder in bowl; mix well.

Using a sharp knife, cut off wing tips from chicken at second joint. Cut through chicken skin along centre back. Using tip of knife, separate flesh from backbone on 1 side of chicken, cutting through thigh joint. Then, following the shape of the

bones, gradually ease flesh away from bone. Holding rib cage away from chicken, carefully cut the breast flesh away from the bone, cutting through wing joint.

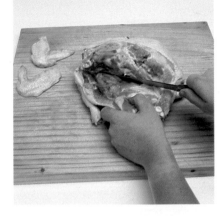

To remove flesh from thigh, hold up 1 thigh with 1 hand. Then, with other hand, cut around top of thigh bone, scrape down bone to next joint, cut around flesh, scrape down to end. Pull bone out and cut away. Repeat process with other half of chicken.

Place chicken with skin side down on bench; spoon mince filling down centre, roll chicken to enclose filling.

Place chicken on greased foil, roll chicken in foil, twist ends tightly.

Place roll on wire rack over baking dish; bake, uncovered, in moderately hot oven 50 minutes. Remove foil from roll, return to oven for 15 minutes or until skin is crisp. Stand 10 minutes before cutting. Serve chicken hot or cold with tomato salsa.
Tomato Salsa: Combine all ingredients in bowl; mix well, cover, refrigerate 2 hours.

Serves 6.

- Recipe can be made a day ahead.
- Storage: Covered, in refrigerator.
- Freeze: Uncooked chicken roll suitable.
- Microwave: Not suitable.

LEFT: Savoury Crepe Stack.
ABOVE: Boned Seasoned Chicken with Tomato Salsa.

Left: Plate from Villa Italiana; tiles from Country Floors. Above: Plate from Clay Things.

LAMB AND EGGPLANT PIE WITH FETA CRUST

1 large (about 500g) eggplant
coarse cooking salt
¼ cup olive oil
2 onions, chopped
1kg minced lamb
410g can tomatoes
⅓ cup tomato paste
2 bay leaves
1 cup water
1 egg, lightly beaten

FETA CRUST
1½ cups self-raising flour
30g butter
¼ cup grated fresh parmesan cheese
80g feta cheese, grated
¾ cup milk, approximately

Cut eggplant into 2cm cubes, sprinkle with salt, stand 30 minutes. Rinse eggplant under cold water; drain well.

Heat 2 tablespoons of the oil in pan, add eggplant and onions, cook, stirring, until onions are soft; remove from pan. Add remaining oil to pan, add mince, cook, stirring, until well browned. Add undrained crushed tomatoes, paste, bay leaves and water, bring to boil, simmer, uncovered, 10 minutes or until thickened, stir in eggplant mixture. Spoon mixture into ovenproof dish (8 cup capacity).

Divide feta dough into 9 portions. Roll each portion into a thin sausage shape. Plait 3 lengths of dough together, place over mince mixture, repeat with remaining dough. Brush dough with egg. Bake, uncovered, in moderate oven about 30 minutes or until dough is browned and mince heated through.

Feta Crust: Sift flour into bowl, rub in butter, stir in cheeses and enough milk to form a soft dough. Knead on lightly floured surface until smooth.

Serves 6.

▦ Mince mixture can be made 3 days ahead.
▦ Storage: Covered, in refrigerator.
▦ Freeze: Mince mixture suitable.
▦ Microwave: Mince mixture suitable.

MEATBALL AND VEGETABLE STIR-FRY WITH PLUM SAUCE

2 tablespoons oil
1 red pepper, chopped
1 green pepper, chopped
¼ Chinese cabbage, shredded
230g can sliced bamboo shoots, drained
½ cup plum sauce
2 teaspoons cornflour
¼ cup water
1 tablespoon light soy sauce
2 tablespoons chopped fresh basil

MINCE WITH ONIONS AND RED WINE

1½kg minced beef
3 (about 450g) onions, chopped
3 (about 360g) carrots, chopped
3 cloves garlic, crushed
2 sprigs fresh thyme
2 bay leaves
2 tablespoons chopped fresh parsley
3 cups dry red wine
6 bacon rashers, chopped
½ cup brandy
½ cup madeira
2 cups water
2 small beef stock cubes
30g butter
250g baby mushrooms
300g baby onions
2 tablespoons cornflour
¼ cup water, extra

Combine mince, chopped onions, carrots, garlic, herbs and wine in bowl, cover, refrigerate 8 hours or overnight.

Strain mince mixture, reserve marinade. Add bacon to large pan, cook, stirring, until crisp; add mince mixture, cook, stirring, until browned. Pour in brandy and madeira; ignite. Add reserved marinade, water and crumbled stock cubes, bring to boil, simmer, covered about 45 minutes, or until mince is tender.

Heat butter in another pan, add mushrooms and baby onions, cook, stirring, until onions are lightly browned. Add mushroom mixture to mince mixture, simmer, covered, 20 minutes or until onions are tender. Stir in blended cornflour and extra water, stir over heat until mixture boils and thickens. Discard thyme and bay leaves. Serve mince with pasta.

Serves 6 to 8.

▦ Recipe can be made a day ahead.
▦ Storage: Covered, in refrigerator.
▦ Freeze: Not suitable.
▦ Microwave: Not suitable.

MEATBALLS
500g minced lamb
4 green shallots, chopped
2 tablespoons oyster sauce
1 egg yolk
1 cup (70g) stale breadcrumbs
1 clove garlic, crushed
1 teaspoon grated fresh ginger
plain flour
oil for shallow-frying

Heat oil in pan or wok, add peppers, stir-fry until just tender, stir in cabbage, bamboo shoots and meatballs, stir-fry until cabbage is tender. Stir in plum sauce,

blended cornflour and water, and soy sauce; stir over heat until mixture boils and thickens; stir in basil.

Meatballs: Combine mince, shallots, sauce, egg yolk, breadcrumbs, garlic and ginger in bowl; mix well. Roll 2 level teaspoons of mixture into balls, toss in flour. Shallow-fry meatballs in hot oil until cooked; drain.

Serves 4.

■ Meatballs can be made a day ahead.
■ Storage: Covered, in refrigerator.
■ Freeze: Meatballs suitable.
■ Microwave: Not suitable.

ABOVE LEFT: Mince with Onions and Red Wine.
ABOVE: From top: Lamb and Eggplant Pie with Feta Crust, Meatball and Vegetable Stir-Fry with Plum Sauce.

Above left: Plate from Villa Italiana; tiles from Country Floors; glass from Mosmania; cloth from Corso de Fiori.

FRUITY MEATLOAF WITH TOMATO APPLE SALSA

600g minced beef
1 onion, finely chopped
¼ cup chopped dried apricots
12 pitted prunes, chopped
1 (about 120g) carrot, grated
½ cup cooked brown rice
2 teaspoons curry powder
¼ cup chopped fresh parsley
3 eggs, lightly beaten

TOMATO APPLE SALSA
1 tablespoon oil
1 apple, finely chopped
2 (about 260g) tomatoes, peeled,
    seeded, chopped
¼ cup brown vinegar
¼ cup water
1 teaspoon sugar
2 tablespoons chopped fresh parsley

Combine all ingredients in bowl; mix well. Press mixture into greased 14cm x 21cm loaf pan. Bake, uncovered, in moderate oven about 1 hour or until firm. Drain away excess liquid, stand 10 minutes before serving. Serve with tomato apple salsa.
Tomato Apple Salsa: Heat oil in pan, add apple, cook, stirring, until just tender. Stir in tomatoes, vinegar, water and sugar, cook, stirring, for about 5 minutes, or until tomatoes are just soft; stir in parsley.

Serves 6.

■ Recipe can be made a day ahead.
■ Storage: Covered, in refrigerator.
■ Freeze: Meatloaf suitable.
■ Microwave: Meatloaf and salsa suitable.

VEGETABLE QUICHE WITH MINCE SHELL

1 tablespoon oil
500g minced beef
1 onion, chopped
1 clove garlic, crushed
1 egg, lightly beaten
¼ cup grated fresh parmesan cheese
1 tablespoon plain flour

FILLING
30g butter
1 medium leek, sliced
2 (about 240g) carrots, grated
1 red pepper, finely chopped
2 (about 200g) zucchini, grated
4 eggs, lightly beaten
⅓ cup grated fresh parmesan cheese
2 tablespoons shredded fresh basil
2 teaspoons seeded mustard

Heat oil in pan, add mince, onion and garlic, cook, stirring, until mince is browned; cool. Stir in egg, cheese and flour; mix well. Press mince mixture over base and side of 23cm pie plate, pour in filling, bake, uncovered, in moderate oven about 50 minutes or until filling is set.

Filling: Heat butter in pan, add leek, cook, stirring, until soft. Add remaining vegetables, stir over heat until vegetables are tender; transfer mixture to bowl, cool. Stir in eggs, cheese, basil and mustard; mix well.

Serves 4 to 6.

■ Quiche best made just before serving.
■ Freeze: Not suitable.
■ Microwave: Not suitable.

PATTIES DIANE WITH MUSHROOM SAUCE

500g minced beef
1 small beef stock cube
1 onion, grated
⅓ cup chopped fresh parsley
2 eggs, lightly beaten
1 cup (100g) packaged breadcrumbs
oil for shallow-frying

MUSHROOM SAUCE
30g butter
2 cloves garlic, crushed
3 green shallots, chopped
150g mushrooms, sliced
¼ cup dry red wine
3 teaspoons Worcestershire sauce
½ cup cream
2 teaspoons cornflour
2 teaspoons water

Combine mince, crumbled stock cube, onion, parsley, eggs and breadcrumbs in bowl. Shape mixture into 8 patties. Shallow-fry patties in hot oil until browned and cooked through. Serve hot with mushroom sauce, and vegetables, if desired.
Mushroom Sauce: Heat butter in pan, add garlic, shallots and mushrooms, cook, stirring, until mushrooms are tender. Add wine, sauce and cream, simmer, uncovered, until reduced by a third. Stir in blended cornflour and water, stir until sauce boils and thickens.

Serves 4.

■ Recipe can be made a day ahead.
■ Storage: Covered, in refrigerator.
■ Freeze: Uncooked patties suitable.
■ Microwave: Not suitable.

Clockwise from left: Vegetable Quiche with Mince Shell, Patties Diane with Mushroom Sauce, Fruity Meatloaf with Tomato Apple Salsa.

China from Villeroy & Boch.

MINI BEEF WELLINGTONS

600g minced beef
1 cup (70g) stale breadcrumbs
3 green shallots, chopped
1 tablespoon tomato paste
2 eggs
1 tablespoon oil
125g liver and peppercorn pate
2 baby mushrooms, sliced
4 sheets ready-rolled puff pastry
1 egg, lightly beaten, extra

MUSHROOM SAUCE
90g butter
250g baby mushrooms, sliced
2½ tablespoons plain flour
1¾ cups water
¼ cup dry red wine
1 teaspoon beef stock powder
2 teaspoons Worcestershire sauce
1 tablespoon tomato paste

Combine mince, breadcrumbs, shallots, paste and eggs in bowl; mix well. Shape mixture into 4 loaves. Heat oil in pan, cook loaves, turning carefully until browned all over. Drain on absorbent paper; cool.

Beat pate in small bowl until smooth, spread loaves with pate, top with mushrooms, press on firmly.

Cut 4cm strip from each sheet of pastry, reserve for decoration.

Place 1 loaf upside down on centre of each pastry sheet, brush edges with extra egg, roll up to form a parcel, pressing edges firmly to seal. With seam side down, decorate with reserved pastry strips; brush with more extra egg. Place parcels on lightly greased oven tray. Bake in moderate oven about 40 minutes or until pastry is browned. Serve parcels with mushroom sauce.

Mushroom Sauce: Heat butter in pan, add mushrooms, cook, stirring, until mushrooms are just tender. Stir in flour, stir over heat until mixture is combined. Remove from heat, gradually stir in water, wine, stock powder, sauce and paste; stir over heat until sauce boils and thickens.

Serves 4.

▦ Recipe can be prepared a day ahead.
▦ Storage: Covered, in refrigerator.
▦ Freeze: Uncooked parcels suitable.
▦ Microwave: Sauce suitable.

SWEET AND SOUR MEATBALLS

¼ cup white rice
500g minced pork and veal
1 clove garlic, crushed
1 egg
2 teaspoons dry sherry
2 teaspoons light soy sauce
plain flour
oil for deep-frying

SWEET AND SOUR SAUCE
450g can pineapple pieces
  in heavy syrup
1 red pepper, chopped
2 teaspoons brown sugar
2 tablespoons light soy sauce
2 tablespoons white vinegar
1 tablespoon cornflour
2 tablespoons water
1 tablespoon chopped fresh parsley

RIGHT: Mini Beef Wellingtons.
FAR RIGHT: From top: Pork and Veal Cannelloni, Sweet and Sour Meatballs.

Add rice to pan of boiling water, boil, un-covered, until just tender; drain.

Combine rice, mince, garlic, egg, sherry and sauce in bowl; mix well. Roll level tablespoons of mixture into balls, toss meatballs in flour, shake away excess flour. Deep-fry meatballs in hot oil until well browned; drain on absorbent paper. Add meatballs to sweet and sour sauce, stir over heat until heated through.

Sweet and Sour Sauce: Drain pineapple, reserve syrup. Combine reserved syrup, pepper, sugar, sauce and vinegar in pan. Stir in blended cornflour and water, stir over heat until sauce boils and thickens. Add pineapple pieces and parsley, stir until heated through.

Serves 4.

- Recipe can be made a day ahead.
- Storage: Covered, in refrigerator.
- Freeze: Not suitable.
- Microwave: Sauce suitable.

PORK AND VEAL CANNELLONI

8 cannelloni tubes
50g butter
1 red Spanish onion, chopped
2 cloves garlic, crushed
350g minced pork and veal
50g mushrooms, chopped
pinch nutmeg
2 tablespoons grated parmesan
cheese
30g butter, extra

SAUCE
400g can tomatoes
5 green shallots, chopped
1 clove garlic, crushed
1 tablespoon chopped fresh basil

Add cannelloni to pan of boiling water, boil, uncovered, until just tender; drain.

Heat butter in pan, add onion and garlic, cook, stirring, until onion is soft. Add mince, cook, stirring, until well browned, add mushrooms and nutmeg, stir until combined; cool.

Fill each cannelloni tube with mince mixture, place in single layer in greased shallow ovenproof dish (6 cup capacity). Pour sauce over cannelloni, sprinkle with cheese, dot with extra butter. Bake, un-covered, in moderate oven about 30 minutes or until lightly browned.

Sauce: Combine undrained crushed tomatoes with remaining ingredients in pan, bring to boil, simmer, uncovered, until reduced by half.

Serves 4.

- Recipe can be made a day ahead.
- Storage: Covered, in refrigerator.
- Freeze: Not suitable.
- Microwave: Cannelloni suitable.

POTATO GNOCCHI WITH MEAT SAUCE

4 large (about 800g) old potatoes
1 egg, lightly beaten
1½ cups plain flour, approximately
½ cup grated fresh parmesan cheese

MEAT SAUCE
1 tablespoon olive oil
1 onion, chopped
1 clove garlic, crushed
750g minced pork and veal
250g mushrooms, chopped
2 x 410g cans tomatoes
2 tablespoons tomato paste
2 teaspoons chicken stock powder
2 tablespoons chopped fresh basil
2 teaspoons chopped fresh oregano
1 teaspoon sugar

Boil, steam or microwave potatoes until soft; drain. Mash potatoes finely in large bowl, stir in egg and enough flour to form a soft dough. Knead dough on lightly floured surface until smooth. Roll level teaspoons of mixture into balls, shape with fork. Add gnocchi to large pan of boiling water in batches, simmer, uncovered, about 3 minutes or until gnocchi rise to surface; drain. Serve gnocchi with meat sauce, serve sprinkled with cheese.

Meat Sauce: Heat oil in pan, add onion, garlic and mince, cook, stirring, until mince is browned. Add mushrooms, cook, stirring, until mushrooms are tender. Stir in undrained crushed tomatoes, paste, stock powder, herbs and sugar. Bring to boil, simmer, uncovered, until mixture is cooked and thickened.

Serves 4 to 6.

■ Recipe can be prepared a day ahead.
■ Storage: Covered, in refrigerator.
■ Freeze: Sauce suitable.
■ Microwave: Gnocchi suitable.

LAMB POTATO POTS

2 tablespoons oil
30g butter
3 large (600g) potatoes, thinly sliced
1 tablespoon oil, extra
1 onion, chopped
1 clove garlic, crushed
600g minced lamb
410g can tomatoes
2 tablespoons tomato paste
2 teaspoons chopped fresh rosemary
2 teaspoons chopped fresh oregano
2 teaspoons chopped fresh thyme
1 small beef stock cube
½ cup grated fresh parmesan cheese

SAUCE
40g butter
2 tablespoons plain flour
1 cup milk

Heat oil and butter in large pan, add potatoes in several batches, cook until lightly browned on both sides. Drain on absorbent paper.

SEASONED ROLLED VEAL WITH RED PEPPERS

2 red peppers
750g piece veal topside
2 tablespoons olive oil

BASIL SEASONING
500g minced pork and veal
½ cup stale breadcrumbs
½ cup fresh grated parmesan cheese
½ cup shredded fresh basil leaves

Quarter peppers, remove seeds and membranes. Grill peppers, skin side up, until skin blisters and blackens. Peel skin from peppers.

Flatten veal with meat mallet to large rectangle, spread with basil seasoning. Place peppers over seasoning. Roll up veal from short end, to enclose filling. Secure veal with string at 3cm intervals. Heat oil in baking dish, add veal, brown all over. Bake, uncovered, in moderate oven about 1½ hours or until tender. Stand 5 minutes before serving. Serve hot or cold.

Basil Seasoning: Combine all ingredients in bowl; mix well.

Serves 6.

■ Veal can be prepared a day ahead.
■ Storage: Covered, in refrigerator.
■ Freeze: Seasoned veal suitable.
■ Microwave: Not suitable.

Heat extra oil in pan, add onion, garlic and mince, cook, stirring, until mince is browned. Stir in undrained crushed tomatoes, paste, herbs and crumbled stock cube. Bring to boil, simmer, uncovered, about 3 minutes or until mixture is slightly thickened.

Divide half the potato between 4 ovenproof dishes (1⅓ cup capacity). Divide meat mixture between dishes, top with remaining potato, then sauce; sprinkle with cheese. Bake, uncovered, in moderate oven about 30 minutes or until heated through.

Sauce: Melt butter in pan, stir in flour, stir until bubbling. Remove from heat, gradually stir in milk; stir over heat until mixture boils and thickens.

Serves 4.

- Recipe can be made a day ahead.
- Storage: Covered, in refrigerator.
- Freeze: Not suitable.
- Microwave: Not suitable.

LAMB AND BEETROOT BAKE

3 medium (about 450g) beetroot
2 large (about 400g) potatoes, thinly sliced
2 tablespoons oil
700g minced lamb
2 cloves garlic, crushed
2 teaspoons caraway seeds
1 teaspoon ground cinnamon
⅓ cup cornflour
1 cup milk
300g carton sour cream
2 tablespoons lemon juice

Boil, steam or microwave beetroot until tender; drain, cool. Remove skin from beetroot, slice beetroot thickly.

Place potatoes in base of lightly greased ovenproof dish (6 cup capacity).

Heat oil in pan, add mince and garlic, cook, stirring, until mince is well browned, add spices, cook, stirring occasionally, until liquid is evaporated. Spoon mince mixture over potatoes, top with beetroot.

Blend cornflour with milk in pan, stir over heat until mixture boils and thickens; remove from heat, stir in sour cream and lemon juice. Pour cream mixture over beetroot, place dish on oven tray, bake, uncovered, in moderate oven about 1 hour or until browned.

Serves 4 to 6.

- Recipe can be made a day ahead.
- Storage: Covered, in refrigerator.
- Freeze: Not suitable.
- Microwave: Not suitable.

LEFT: From left: Seasoned Rolled Veal with Red Peppers, Potato Gnocchi with Meat Sauce.
BELOW: From left: Lamb and Beetroot Bake, Lamb Potato Pots.

Left: Pottery from Clay Things. Below: China from Wedgwood; tea-towel from Between the Sheets.

VEGETABLE AND MINCE POTS WITH CRUNCHY TOPPING

250g packet frozen spinach, thawed
60g butter
1 medium leek, sliced
250g cauliflower, chopped
150g mushrooms, sliced
¼ cup dry white wine

FILLING
1 tablespoon oil
500g minced beef
1 small beef stock cube
300g can Mushroom Supreme
2 green shallots, chopped

TOPPING
4 slices bread
50g butter, melted
½ cup grated tasty cheese

Squeeze spinach to remove excess liquid. Heat butter in pan, add leek, cauliflower and mushrooms, cook, stirring, until leek and cauliflower are just soft, add spinach and wine, stir until heated through. Spoon mixture into 4 ovenproof dishes (1½ cup capacity). Spoon over filling, sprinkle with topping. Place dishes on oven tray. Bake, uncovered, in moderate oven about 15 minutes or until browned and heated through.

Filling: Heat oil in pan, add mince, cook, stirring, until well browned. Add crumbled stock cube, Mushroom Supreme and shallots, cook, stirring, until hot.

Topping: Remove crusts from bread, cut bread into small cubes. Combine bread, butter and cheese in bowl; mix gently.

Serves 4.

- Recipe can be made 2 days ahead.
- Storage: Covered, in refrigerator.
- Freeze: Suitable.
- Microwave: Vegetables and filling suitable.

PASTA WITH MINCE AND FETA CHEESE

500g lasagnette
1 tablespoon olive oil
500g minced beef
1 clove garlic, crushed
1 onion, chopped
½ teaspoon chilli powder
1 small beef stock cube
400g can tomatoes
½ cup water
½ cup black olives, halved
1 tablespoon chopped fresh coriander
250g feta cheese, chopped

Add pasta to large pan of boiling water, boil, uncovered, until just tender; drain.

Meanwhile, heat oil in pan, add mince, garlic, onion and chilli powder, cook, stirring, until mince is well browned. Stir in crumbled stock cube, undrained crushed tomatoes, water and olives. Bring to boil, simmer, uncovered, about 5 minutes or

until mixture is slightly thickened. Stir in coriander and cheese, serve over pasta.

Serves 4.

- ▨ Recipe best made just before serving.
- ▨ Freeze: Not suitable.
- ▨ Microwave: Pasta suitable.

MINCE AND MORTADELLA LOAF WITH MUSHROOM SAUCE

750g minced beef
½ cup stale breadcrumbs
1 onion, chopped
1 egg, lightly beaten
2 cloves garlic, crushed
⅓ cup grated fresh parmesan cheese
2 tablespoons chopped fresh basil
⅓ cup chopped black olives
150g sliced mortadella, chopped

MUSHROOM SAUCE
2 tablespoons oil
1 onion, sliced
250g mushrooms, sliced
410g can tomatoes
1 tablespoon tomato paste
1 teaspoon sugar
2 tablespoons dry red wine

Combine all ingredients in bowl; mix well. Press mince mixture firmly into lightly greased 14cm x 21cm loaf pan. Bake meatloaf, uncovered, in moderate oven about 1 hour or until firm; drain. Cover pan; stand meatloaf 15 minutes before slicing. Serve with mushroom sauce.
Mushroom Sauce: Heat oil in pan, add onion and mushrooms, cook, stirring, until onion is soft. Stir in undrained crushed tomatoes, paste, sugar and wine, bring to boil, simmer, uncovered, until sauce is thickened slightly.

Serves 6.

- ▨ Recipe can be made a day ahead.
- ▨ Storage: Covered, in refrigerator.
- ▨ Freeze: Cooked meatloaf suitable.
- ▨ Microwave: Not suitable.

MINCE AND PASTA MEATBALLS WITH CHEESE SAUCE

½ cup miniature pasta
1kg minced beef
2 cups (140g) stale breadcrumbs
1 onion, finely chopped
2 cloves garlic, crushed
2 tablespoons tomato paste
1 tablespoon chopped fresh basil
1 tablespoon chopped fresh oregano
1 egg, lightly beaten
oil for deep-frying

CHEESE SAUCE
40g butter
¼ cup plain flour
2 cups milk
1½ cups (190g) grated tasty cheese
½ cup grated fresh parmesan cheese

Add pasta to pan of boiling water, boil, uncovered, until just tender; drain, cool.
Combine pasta, mince, breadcrumbs,

onion, garlic, paste, herbs and egg in bowl; mix well. Shape level tablespoons of mixture into balls. Deep-fry meatballs in hot oil until browned; drain.

Transfer meatballs to shallow ovenproof dish (6 cup capacity), top with cheese sauce. Bake, uncovered, in moderate oven about 30 minutes or until heated through. Sprinkle with chopped parsley and paprika, if desired.
Cheese Sauce: Heat butter in pan, stir in flour, cook, stirring, until mixture is bubbling. Remove from heat, gradually stir in milk, stir over heat until mixture boils and thickens. Stir in cheeses.

Serves 6.

- ▨ Recipe can be made a day ahead.
- ▨ Storage: Covered, in refrigerator.
- ▨ Freeze: Meatballs suitable.
- ▨ Microwave: Cheese sauce suitable.

LEFT: Pasta with Mince and Feta Cheese, Vegetable and Mince Pots with Crunchy Topping.
ABOVE: From top: Mince and Mortadella Loaf with Mushroom Sauce, Mince and Pasta Meatballs with Cheese Sauce.

Above: Plates from Accoutrement; tiles from Country Floors.

CHICKEN, RICE AND MANGO PIE

500g minced chicken
1 onion, chopped
½ teaspoon dried mixed herbs
1 cup (70g) stale breadcrumbs
2 tablespoons mango chutney
⅓ cup flaked almonds

FILLING
15g butter
1 teaspoon sesame oil
1 onion, chopped
⅔ cup brown rice
2 teaspoons chicken stock powder
1½ cups water
½ x 425g can mangoes, drained, chopped
¼ red pepper, chopped
¼ cup frozen peas
2 tablespoons mango chutney
2 teaspoons light soy sauce

Combine mince, onion, herbs, bread-crumbs and chutney in bowl; mix well. Press mince mixture over base and side of greased 25cm pie plate. Bake, un-covered, in moderate oven about 35 minutes or until firm.

Drain off fat using absorbent paper. Return pie case to oven further 5 minutes.

Spoon filling into pie case, sprinkle with almonds. Bake, uncovered, in moderate oven 30 minutes.

Filling: Heat butter and oil in pan, add onion, cook, stirring, until soft; add rice, cook, stirring, 1 minute. Add stock powder and water, bring to boil, stir once, simmer, tightly covered, until rice is tender and liquid absorbed. Stir in mangoes, pepper, peas, chutney and sauce; mix well.

Serves 6.

▩ Recipe can be made a day ahead.
▩ Storage: Covered, in refrigerator.
▩ Freeze: Not suitable.
▩ Microwave: Not suitable.

BEEF AND PARSNIP PIE

5 medium (about 750g) parsnips, chopped
20g butter
2 tablespoons milk

FILLING
1 tablespoon oil
1 onion, chopped
1 (about 120g) carrot, chopped
500g minced beef
410g can tomatoes
¼ cup water
1 small beef stock cube
2 tablespoons tomato paste
½ teaspoon sugar

TOPPING
½ cup stale breadcrumbs
¾ cup grated tasty cheese

Boil, steam or microwave parsnips until tender; drain. Mash parsnips until smooth, stir in butter and milk. Spread mixture over base and side of greased 25cm pie plate. Spread filling over base, sprinkle with top-ping. Bake, uncovered, in moderate oven about 30 minutes or until brown.

Filling: Heat oil in pan, add onion, cook, stirring, until soft. Add carrot and mince, cook, stirring, until mince is browned. Add undrained crushed tomatoes, water, crumbled stock cube, paste and sugar. Bring to boil, simmer, uncovered, about 15 minutes or until liquid is evaporated.

Topping: Combine breadcrumbs and cheese in small bowl.

Serves 4 to 6.

▩ Recipe can be prepared a day ahead.
▩ Storage: Covered, in refrigerator.
▩ Freeze: Suitable.
▩ Microwave: Parsnips suitable.

BEEF WITH CHICK PEAS AND OLIVES

1 tablespoon oil
1 onion, chopped
3 cloves garlic, crushed
700g minced beef
310g can chick peas, rinsed, drained
410g can tomatoes
⅓ cup sultanas
⅓ cup (about 12) green olives, halved
1 teaspoon ground cinnamon
½ teaspoon ground allspice
pinch cayenne pepper
2 bay leaves
2 small beef stock cubes
2 tablespoons tomato paste

Heat oil in pan, add onion and garlic, cook, stirring, until onion is soft, add mince, cook, stirring, until mince is well browned. Stir in chick peas, undrained crushed tomatoes, sultanas, olives, spices, cayenne, bay leaves, crumbled stock cubes and paste. Bring to boil, simmer, uncovered, until mixture is thick. Discard bay leaves before serving.

Serves 6.

▩ Recipe can be made a day ahead.
▩ Storage: Covered, in refrigerator.
▩ Freeze: Suitable.
▩ Microwave: Suitable.

BELOW: Chicken, Rice and Mango Pie.
RIGHT: From top: Beef with Chick Peas and Olives, Beef and Parsnip Pie.

Below: Plate from Modern Living.

BEEF KEBABS WITH CUCUMBER SAUCE

700g minced beef
1 onion, chopped
2 egg whites
½ teaspoon ground allspice
1 teaspoon chopped fresh dill
¼ cup oil

CUCUMBER SAUCE
1 long thin green cucumber
300g carton sour cream
1 tablespoon chopped fresh dill
1 teaspoon beef stock powder
1 tablespoon dry sherry

Process beef, onion, egg whites, allspice and dill until combined. Roll level tablespoons of mixture into balls, flatten slightly, cover, refrigerate 30 minutes.

Thread meatballs onto 12 skewers. Heat oil in pan, add kebabs, cook until brown. Serve with cucumber sauce.

Cucumber Sauce: Cut cucumber lengthways, remove seeds, slice cucumber thinly. Combine sour cream, dill, stock powder and sherry in pan, cook, stirring, until well combined and heated through; stir in cucumber.

Serves 4 to 6.

■ Recipe can be prepared a day ahead.
■ Storage: Covered, in refrigerator.
■ Freeze: Uncooked kebabs suitable.
■ Microwave: Cucumber sauce suitable.

CHILLI MINCE CREPES

½ cup plain flour
1 egg, lightly beaten
1 cup milk
1 teaspoon oil
pinch paprika

FILLING
1 tablespoon oil
1 onion, chopped
1 clove garlic, crushed
500g minced beef
½ teaspoon Mexican chilli seasoning
410g can tomatoes
2 tablespoons tomato paste
310g can red kidney beans, rinsed, drained

CHEESE TOPPING
30g butter
2 tablespoons plain flour
1 cup milk
½ cup grated tasty cheese

Sift flour into bowl, gradually stir in combined egg, milk and oil, beat until smooth (or, blend or process all ingredients until smooth). Cover, stand 30 minutes.

Pour 2 to 3 tablespoons of batter into heated greased heavy-based pan, cook until browned underneath. Turn crepe, brown other side. Repeat with remaining batter. You will need 8 crepes.

Divide filling among crepes, roll to enclose filling, place in single layer in greased shallow flameproof dish. Pour cheese topping over crepes, sprinkle with paprika. Grill until lightly browned.

Filling: Heat oil in pan, add onion and garlic, cook, stirring, until onion is soft. Add mince, cook, stirring, until browned. Add seasoning, undrained crushed tomatoes and paste, bring to boil, simmer, uncovered, about 20 minutes or until thick. Stir in beans.

Cheese Topping: Melt butter in pan, stir in flour, stir over heat until bubbling. Remove from heat, gradually stir in milk, stir over heat until sauce boils and thickens. Remove from heat, stir in cheese.

Serves 4.

■ Crepes and filling can be prepared a day ahead.
■ Storage: Covered, in refrigerator.
■ Freeze: Crepes suitable.
■ Microwave: Not suitable.

DRY BEEF AND POTATO CURRY

1 tablespoon oil
1kg minced beef
1 tablespoon plain flour
410g can tomatoes
1 cinnamon stick
2 large (about 400g) potatoes, chopped
1 cup water
¾ cup frozen peas

CURRY PASTE
1 onion, chopped
2 cloves garlic, crushed
1 teaspoon ground cloves
1 teaspoon ground cardamom
1 teaspoon ground fennel
2 teaspoons ground coriander
2 teaspoons ground cumin
1½ tablespoons garam masala
1 tablespoon tomato paste
1 teaspoon grated fresh ginger
¼ cup lemon juice
¼ cup oil
¼ cup water
1 teaspoon sugar

Heat oil in large pan, add curry paste, cook, stirring, until fragrant. Add mince and flour, cook, stirring, until mince changes colour. Add undrained crushed tomatoes and cinnamon stick, simmer, covered, 15 minutes. Add potatoes, water and peas, simmer, covered, 15 minutes or until potatoes are tender.

Curry Paste: Blend or process all ingredients until smooth.

Serves 6.

■ Recipe can be made a day ahead.
■ Storage: Covered, in refrigerator.
■ Freeze: Suitable.
■ Microwave: Not suitable.

Clockwise from left: Beef Kebabs with Cucumber Sauce, Chilli Mince Crepes, Dry Beef and Potato Curry.

HOT POTS WITH CORNMEAL CRUST

1 tablespoon oil
1 onion, finely chopped
1 clove garlic, crushed
1 teaspoon grated fresh ginger
800g minced beef
¼ teaspoon ground cloves
1½ teaspoons ground cinnamon
1 teaspoon curry powder
1 tablespoon plain flour
2½ cups water
½ cup sultanas
½ cup chopped dried apricots
1 tablespoon milk

CORNMEAL CRUST
1 cup self-raising flour
½ cup cornmeal
2 teaspoons butter
1 small red pepper, finely chopped
2 tablespoons finely chopped fresh chives
1 tablespoon chopped fresh parsley
½ cup milk, approximately

Heat oil in pan, add onion, garlic and ginger, cook, stirring, until onion is soft. Add mince, cloves, cinnamon, curry powder and flour, cook, stirring, until mince changes colour. Stir in water, bring to boil, simmer, covered, 20 minutes, stir in sultanas and apricots, simmer, covered, further 10 minutes. Divide mixture between 4 ovenproof dishes (1½ cup capacity).

Roll cornmeal dough on lightly floured surface to a 20cm x 30cm rectangle, roll up from long side like a Swiss roll; cut into 1cm slices. Place slices on filling, brush with milk. Place dishes on oven tray, bake, uncovered, in moderately hot oven about 30 minutes or until crust is browned.
Cornmeal Crust: Sift flour and cornmeal into bowl, rub in butter. Stir in pepper, chives and parsley. Stir in enough milk to make a soft dough. Knead dough on lightly floured surface until smooth.

Serves 4.

- Recipe can be made a day ahead.
- Storage: Covered, in refrigerator.
- Freeze: Not suitable.
- Microwave: Not suitable.

LASAGNE

200g packet instant lasagne pasta sheets
½ cup grated fresh parmesan cheese

MEAT SAUCE
1 tablespoon oil
1 onion, chopped
2 cloves garlic, crushed
500g minced beef
2 x 410g can tomatoes
¼ cup tomato paste
¼ cup dry red wine
1 teaspoon sugar
¼ cup shredded fresh basil

CHEESE SAUCE
30g butter
2½ tablespoons plain flour
2 cups milk
½ cup cream
1 cup (125g) grated tasty cheese
¼ teaspoon ground nutmeg

Spread one third of meat sauce over base of greased 23cm slab pan. Top with one third of pasta sheets and one third of cheese sauce. Continue layering, ending with cheese sauce. Sprinkle with cheese; bake, uncovered, in moderate oven about 1 hour or until pasta is tender.
Meat Sauce: Heat oil in pan, add onion, garlic and mince, cook, stirring, until mince is well browned. Stir in undrained crushed tomatoes, paste, wine and sugar. Bring to boil, simmer, uncovered, until sauce is thick; stir in basil.
Cheese Sauce: Melt butter in pan, stir in flour, stir over heat until mixture is dry and grainy. Remove from heat, gradually stir in milk and cream, stir over heat until sauce boils and thickens. Remove from heat, stir in cheese and nutmeg.

Serves 4 to 6.

- Lasagne can be made a day ahead.
- Storage: Covered, in refrigerator.
- Freeze: Suitable.
- Microwave: Suitable.

BEEF RISOTTO

90g butter
1 onion, finely chopped
1 clove garlic, crushed
500g minced beef
2 small beef stock cubes
1¼ cups water
400g can tomatoes
2 tablespoons tomato paste
1 cup long grain rice
½ cup frozen peas
¼ cup shredded fresh basil
½ cup grated fresh parmesan cheese

Heat butter in pan, add onion and garlic, cook, stirring, until onion is soft. Add mince, cook, stirring, until mince is browned. Stir in crumbled stock cubes, water, undrained crushed tomatoes, paste and rice. Bring to boil, simmer, covered, stirring occasionally, until almost all liquid is absorbed. Add peas, cover, cook until rice is tender. Remove from heat, stir in basil and half the cheese. Serve sprinkled with remaining cheese.

Serves 4.

- Recipe best made just before serving.
- Freeze: Not suitable.
- Microwave: Not suitable.

LEFT: From back: Hot Pots with Cornmeal Crust, Lasagne.
ABOVE: Beef Risotto.

EGGPLANT CAKE WITH TOMATO SAUCE

2 tablespoons packaged breadcrumbs
2 large (about 1kg) eggplants
coarse cooking salt
1 tablespoon olive oil
440g can new potatoes, drained, sliced

MINCE LAYER
2 teaspoons oil
500g minced beef
1 clove garlic, crushed
½ teaspoon ground cumin
2 tablespoons plain flour
400g can tomatoes
1 tablespoon tomato paste
1 teaspoon sugar
1 egg white, lightly beaten

TOMATO SAUCE
1 tablespoon olive oil
1 medium leek, chopped
1 clove garlic, crushed
2 large (about 500g) tomatoes, seeded, chopped
¼ cup dry red wine
¼ cup tomato sauce
2 tablespoons shredded fresh basil

Grease deep 23cm round cake pan. Sprinkle with breadcrumbs.

Cut eggplants into 5mm thick slices, sprinkle with salt, stand 20 minutes. Rinse slices under cold water; drain, pat dry with absorbent paper. Brush both sides of slices with oil, grill until lightly browned on both sides; drain on absorbent paper.

Line base and side of prepared pan with two-thirds of the eggplants. Spoon in half the mince mixture, top with potatoes and remaining mince mixture, then remaining eggplants. Cover pan with foil, bake in moderate oven about 1 hour or until firm. Stand 5 minutes before turning out. Serve hot or cold with tomato sauce.

Mince Layer: Heat oil in pan, add mince, garlic and cumin, cook, stirring, until mince is well browned. Remove from heat, stir in flour, then undrained crushed tomatoes, paste and sugar, stir over heat until mixture boils and thickens; cool. Stir in egg white.

Tomato Sauce: Heat oil in pan, add leek and garlic, cook, stirring, until leek is soft. Add tomatoes and wine, bring to boil, simmer, uncovered, until reduced by one third; add sauce and basil, stir until hot.

Serves 6.

- Recipe can be made a day ahead.
- Storage: Covered, in refrigerator.
- Freeze: Not suitable.
- Microwave: Tomato sauce suitable.

RIGHT: Steak and Kidney Pudding.
FAR RIGHT: Eggplant Cake with Tomato Sauce.

Far right: Plate from Mikasa Tableware.

STEAK AND KIDNEY PUDDING

You need to buy about 300g fresh suet for this recipe.
3 cups self-raising flour
2 cups (150g) grated fresh suet
1 cup water
⅓ cup water, extra

FILLING
1 tablespoon oil
1 onion, chopped
1 clove garlic, crushed
1kg minced beef
250g lambs' kidneys, chopped
125g mushrooms, chopped
2 small beef stock cubes
1 cup water
2 tablespoons tomato paste
2 tablespoons chutney
1 tablespoon Worcestershire sauce

Sift flour into bowl, add suet and water, mix to a soft dough, turn onto floured surface, knead until smooth. Roll two-thirds of dough large enough to line greased 8 cup capacity pudding steamer.

Spoon filling into pastry case, pour extra water over filling. Roll remaining pastry large enough to cover filling. Brush top edge of pastry with water, press on pastry top, seal and trim edges.

Cover pudding with greased foil, secure with string or lid. Place steamer in large pan with enough boiling water to come halfway up side of steamer; boil, covered, 2 hours; replenish water with boiling water as it evaporates. Stand pudding 10 minutes before turning out.

Filling: Heat oil in pan, add onion and garlic, cook, stirring, until onion is soft. Add mince, cook, stirring, until well browned. Stir in kidneys, mushrooms, crumbled stock cubes, water, paste, chutney and sauce; bring to boil, cool.

Serves 6.

- Filling can be prepared a day ahead.
- Storage: Covered, in refrigerator.
- Freeze: Suitable.
- Microwave: Not suitable.

BONED SEASONED LOIN OF VEAL

1kg loin of veal, boned
1 clove garlic, crushed
6 slices prosciutto
6 leaves English spinach
20g butter
1 medium leek, finely chopped
250g minced chicken
1 tablespoon chopped fresh basil
¼ red pepper
1 small (about 80g) carrot
50g green beans
2 tablespoons olive oil
1 teaspoon cracked black
   peppercorns
1 tablespoon plain flour
½ cup dry white wine
½ cup water
1 teaspoon chicken stock powder
1 teaspoon seeded mustard
¼ cup cream

Unroll veal, cut through fleshy part to form a flap, open out flap so that it forms 1 large piece of veal.

Flatten veal with meat mallet. Rub cut side of veal with garlic, line with prosciutto and spinach leaves.

Heat butter in pan, add leek, cook, stirring, until soft; cool. Combine leek, mince and basil in bowl; mix well. Place mince mixture over prosciutto.

Cut pepper and carrot into thin strips. Boil, steam or microwave pepper, carrot and beans until just tender; drain, rinse under cold water, drain, pat dry with absorbent paper. Place vegetables over mince mixture.

Roll up veal firmly to enclose filling, secure at 2cm intervals with string.

Rub veal with 1 tablespoon of the oil, sprinkle with peppercorns. Heat remaining oil in ovenproof dish, add veal, bake, uncovered, in hot oven 10 minutes;

reduce heat to moderate, bake about further 50 minutes or until veal is tender.

Transfer veal to serving dish, reserve pan juices. Cover veal with foil. Stir flour into reserved pan juices, stir over heat until mixture is lightly browned. Remove from heat; gradually stir in wine, water, stock powder, mustard and cream. Stir over heat until sauce boils and thickens; strain. Serve veal with sauce.

Serves 6 to 8.

- Veal can be prepared a day ahead.
- Storage: Covered, in refrigerator
- Freeze: Not suitable.
- Microwave: Vegetables suitable.

CREAMY CHICKEN AND POTATO BAKE

1 tablespoon oil
500g minced chicken
200g mushrooms, chopped
300ml carton thickened cream
1 teaspoon cornflour
1 tablespoon water
500g potatoes, sliced
30g butter
1 small red pepper
1 small green pepper
30g butter, extra
1 small onion, sliced
½ small leek, sliced
1 tablespoon chopped fresh parsley

Heat oil in pan, add mince, cook, stirring, until changed in colour. Add mushrooms, cook, stirring, until liquid is evaporated. Stir in cream and blended cornflour and water, stir over heat until mixture boils and thickens. Spoon mixture into ovenproof dish (6 cup capacity).

Boil, steam or microwave potatoes until almost tender, rinse potatoes under cold water; drain on absorbent paper. Heat half the butter in pan, add half the potatoes, cook until browned and just tender; repeat with remaining butter and potatoes.

Cut peppers into thin strips. Heat extra butter in same pan, add peppers, onion and leek, cook, stirring, until leek is soft. Return potatoes to pan, combine gently.

Spoon potato mixture over mince mixture. Bake, covered, in moderate oven about 15 minutes or until heated through. Sprinkle with parsley before serving.

Serves 4 to 6.

- Recipe can be prepared 3 hours ahead.
- Storage: Covered, in refrigerator.
- Freeze: Not suitable.
- Microwave: Not suitable.

CHICKEN FRICASSEE WITH DILL SHORTCAKES

5 bacon rashers, chopped
750g minced chicken
60g butter
3 green shallots, chopped
250g mushrooms, chopped
1/3 cup plain flour
2 cups water
2 small chicken stock cubes
3/4 cup cream
1 cup (125g) frozen green beans
1 tablespoon lemon juice
2 tablespoons chopped fresh dill
1 tablespoon seeded mustard

DILL SHORTCAKES
3/4 cup plain flour
1 cup self-raising flour
1/2 teaspoon bicarbonate of soda
1 small chicken stock cube
1/2 teaspoon sugar
2 tablespoons chopped fresh dill
90g butter, chopped
2/3 cup sour cream
1/4 cup milk, approximately

Cook bacon in pan until crisp, add mince, stir over heat until mince is changed in colour; remove from heat; drain.

Heat butter in pan, add shallots and mushrooms, cook, stirring, until mushrooms are soft. Stir in flour, stir over heat until bubbling. Remove from heat, stir in water and crumbled stock cubes. Stir over heat until sauce boils and thickens. Stir in chicken mixture, cream, beans, juice, dill and mustard. Stir over heat until heated through, serve with dill shortcakes.

Dill Shortcakes: Sift dry ingredients into bowl, stir in crumbled stock cube, sugar and dill, rub in butter. Stir in cream and enough milk to form a soft sticky dough. Cover, refrigerate 30 minutes.

Roll dough on floured surface until 1cm thick. Cut 9cm rounds from dough. Place rounds on greased oven tray, bake in hot oven about 15 minutes or until browned.

Serves 4 to 6.

- Recipe can be prepared a day ahead.
- Storage: Covered, in refrigerator.
- Freeze: Not suitable.
- Microwave: Chicken mixture suitable.

Clockwise from left: Boned Seasoned Loin of Veal, Creamy Chicken and Potato Bake, Chicken Fricassee with Dill Shortcakes.

China from Wedgwood.

SHORTCAKES WITH CHILLI CON CARNE

1 tablespoon oil
2 onions, chopped
2 cloves garlic, crushed
1kg minced beef
1 tablespoon ground cumin
½ teaspoon chilli powder
1 teaspoon dried chilli flakes
2 tablespoons paprika
1 tablespoon dried oregano leaves
2 (about 240g) carrots, finely sliced
410g can tomatoes
1 small beef stock cube
1½ cups water
¼ cup cider vinegar
310g can red kidney beans, rinsed, drained
1 green pepper, chopped

SHORTCAKES

1 cup self-raising flour
½ cup plain flour
½ teaspoon bicarbonate of soda
40g butter
1½ cups (190g) grated tasty cheese
4 pickled jalapeno peppers, finely chopped
1 cup sour cream

Heat oil in pan, add onions and garlic, cook, stirring, until onion is soft. Add mince, cook, stirring, until well browned. Stir in cumin, chilli powder and flakes, paprika and oregano, cook, stirring, further 2 minutes. Stir in carrots, undrained crushed tomatoes, crumbled stock cube, water and vinegar. Bring to boil, simmer, covered, 1 hour. Add beans and pepper, simmer, covered, further 15 minutes. Split each shortcake in half, serve filled with mince mixture.

Shortcakes: Sift dry ingredients into bowl, rub in butter. Stir in cheese, peppers and cream. Mix to a firm dough. Knead dough on lightly floured surface until smooth, cover, refrigerate 30 minutes.

Roll dough on lightly floured surface to 2cm thick, cut into 6 x 8cm circles, place on greased oven tray, bake, uncovered, in moderately hot oven, about 25 minutes or until browned.

Serves 6.

■ Recipe can be made a day ahead.
■ Storage: Covered, in refrigerator.
■ Freeze: Not suitable.
■ Microwave: Not suitable.

BELOW: Shortcakes with Chilli Con Carne.
RIGHT: From left: Meatballs with Spinach and Chick Peas, Pastitso.

Below: Plate from Mikasa Tableware.

PASTITSO

500g millerighi pasta
125g butter
1 cup plain flour
1 litre (4 cups) milk
1 cup (80g) coarsely grated fresh parmesan cheese
½ cup grated tasty cheese
1 red pepper, finely chopped
½ teaspoon dried basil leaves
½ teaspoon dried oregano leaves

MEAT SAUCE

2 tablespoons olive oil
2 onions, chopped
1 clove garlic, crushed
750g minced beef
250g mushrooms, sliced
1 green pepper, finely chopped
400g can tomatoes
1 small beef stock cube

Add pasta to large pan of boiling water, boil, uncovered, until just tender; drain, place in bowl.

Heat butter in pan, add flour, stir over heat until bubbling. Remove from heat, gradually stir in milk, stir over heat until mixture boils and thickens. Remove from heat, stir in cheeses.

Stir half the cheese sauce into bowl of pasta, spread over base of greased 21cm x 33cm shallow ovenproof dish. Spoon

over meat sauce, smooth surface. Top with remaining cheese sauce; sprinkle with pepper, basil and oregano. Bake, un-covered, in moderate oven about 30 minutes or until browned.

Meat Sauce: Heat oil in pan, add onions and garlic, cook, stirring, until onions are soft. Add mince, cook, stirring, until browned. Add mushrooms and pepper, cook, stirring, until vegetables are just tender. Add undrained crushed tomatoes and crumbled stock cube, bring to boil, simmer, uncovered, until thick.

Serves 6 to 8.

■ Recipe can be made a day ahead.
■ Storage: Covered, in refrigerator.
■ Freeze: Suitable.
■ Microwave: Pasta suitable.

MEATBALLS WITH SPINACH AND CHICK PEAS

500g minced beef
1 egg, lightly beaten
½ cup packaged breadcrumbs
½ teaspoon dried oregano leaves
plain flour
oil for deep-frying
250g packet frozen spinach
2 x 310g can chick peas, rinsed, drained

TOMATO SAUCE
1 tablespoon olive oil
1 onion, chopped
1 clove garlic, crushed
2 x 410g cans tomatoes
½ cup water
¼ cup tomato paste
1 small beef stock cube
1 teaspoon sugar

Combine mince, egg, breadcrumbs and oregano in bowl; mix well. Roll level tablespoons of mixture into balls, toss in flour; shake away excess flour. Deep-fry meatballs in hot oil until well browned; drain on absorbent paper.

Heat frozen spinach in pan until thawed and liquid is evaporated. Add spinach, chick peas and meatballs to tomato sauce, stir until heated through.

Tomato Sauce: Heat oil in pan, add onion and garlic, cook, stirring, until onion is soft, add undrained crushed tomatoes, water, tomato paste, crumbled stock cube and sugar, bring to boil, simmer, uncovered, 20 minutes.

Serves 4.

■ Recipe can be made a day ahead.
■ Storage: Covered in refrigerator.
■ Freeze: Suitable.
■ Microwave: Not suitable.

NUGGET PUMPKINS WITH CHICKEN AND SPINACH SAUCE

1 tablespoon oil
2 cloves garlic, crushed
2 tablespoons pine nuts
¼ teaspoon ground fennel
¾ teaspoon turmeric
1 teaspoon ground cumin
500g minced chicken
¼ cup currants
400g can tomatoes
4 medium golden nugget pumpkins

SPINACH SAUCE
30g butter
1 small onion, sliced
1 teaspoon cumin seeds, crushed
**¼ bunch (10 leaves) English
    spinach, shredded**
1 small chicken stock cube
300ml carton cream
1 teaspoon cornflour
½ cup water

Heat oil in pan, add garlic, pine nuts, fennel, turmeric and cumin; cook, stirring, until fragrant. Add mince, cook, stirring, until changed in colour. Stir in currants and undrained crushed tomatoes.

Cut tops from pumpkins, carefully scoop out seeds; discard seeds. Fill pumpkins with mince mixture, replace tops. Place pumpkins in ovenproof dish, add enough boiling water to come 1cm up sides of pumpkins; bake, covered, in moderately hot oven about 50 minutes or until pumpkins are tender. Serve pumpkins with spinach sauce.

Spinach Sauce: Heat butter in pan, add onion and cumin seeds; cook, stirring, until onion is soft. Add spinach, crumbled stock cube and cream, bring to boil. Stir in blended cornflour and water, stir over heat until mixture boils and thickens.

Serves 4.

- Recipe can be prepared 2 days ahead.
- Storage: Covered, in refrigerator.
- Freeze: Not suitable.
- Microwave: Suitable.

LEFT: Nugget Pumpkins with Chicken and Spinach Sauce.
ABOVE RIGHT: Meatballs with Sweet Pepper Sauce.

Left: Picnic rug from Between the Sheets.

MEATBALLS WITH SWEET PEPPER SAUCE

1 cup (70g) stale breadcrumbs
¼ cup milk
500g minced beef
1 small onion, chopped
2 tablespoons chopped fresh parsley
1 teaspoon dried mixed herbs
1 egg, lightly beaten
2 tablespoons oil

SWEET PEPPER SAUCE
1 tablespoon oil
1 small onion, chopped
1 red pepper, chopped
1 green pepper, chopped
2 sticks celery, chopped
1 teaspoon paprika
¼ cup tomato paste
1 teaspoon beef stock powder
1 cup water

Combine breadcrumbs and milk in bowl; stand 5 minutes. Combine breadcrumb mixture, mince, onion, herbs and egg in bowl; mix well. Shape level tablespoons of mixture into balls.

Heat oil in pan, add meatballs, cook, shaking pan occasionally until meatballs are browned; drain on absorbent paper. Transfer meatballs to shallow ovenproof dish (4 cup capacity), top with sweet pepper sauce. Bake, covered, in moderate oven about 30 minutes or until hot.

Sweet Pepper Sauce: Heat oil in pan, add onion, peppers and celery, cook, stirring, until onion is soft. Stir in paprika, paste, stock powder and water; stir over heat until well combined.

Serves 4.

- Recipe can be made a day ahead.
- Storage: Covered, in refrigerator.
- Freeze: Not suitable.
- Microwave: Sweet pepper sauce suitable.

95

MEATBALLS WITH SOUR CREAM AND GHERKINS

750g minced beef
1 egg, lightly beaten
1½ teaspoons caraway seeds, crushed
1 onion, grated
2 teaspoons paprika
1½ cups (110g) stale breadcrumbs
¼ cup water
plain flour
oil for deep-frying
2 x 300g cartons sour cream
½ cup sliced dill gherkins
1 teaspoon dried dill leaves
½ teaspoon paprika, extra
1 cup water, extra

Combine mince, egg, seeds, onion, paprika, breadcrumbs and water in bowl; mix well. Roll level tablespoons of mixture into balls, toss in flour; shake away excess flour. Deep-fry meatballs in hot oil until browned and cooked through; drain on absorbent paper.

Combine sour cream, gherkins, dill, extra paprika and extra water in pan, stir over heat without boiling until heated through. Add meatballs, stir until hot. Serve with rice and vegetables, and sprinkled with a little paprika, if desired.

Serves 6 to 8.

- Meatballs can be prepared a day ahead.
- Storage: Covered, in refrigerator.
- Freeze: Uncooked meatballs suitable.
- Microwave: Not suitable.

BEEF AND BEANS WITH POLENTA TRIANGLES

1 tablespoon oil
1 onion, chopped
500g minced beef
½ teaspoon ground allspice
410g can tomatoes
450g can three-bean mix, rinsed, drained
½ teaspoon seasoned pepper
½ cup water
1 teaspoon beef stock powder
2 tablespoons tomato paste
1 tablespoon chopped fresh parsley

POLENTA
1¾ cups water
½ cup polenta
⅔ cup coarsely grated fresh parmesan cheese
1 egg, lightly beaten
20g butter
plain flour
oil for shallow-frying

Heat oil in pan, add onion, mince and spice, cook, stirring, until mince is browned. Add undrained crushed tomatoes, beans, pepper, water, stock powder and paste. Bring to boil, simmer, covered, until thickened slightly; stir in parsley. Serve with polenta triangles.

Polenta: Line 2 x 8cm x 26cm bar cake pans with plastic wrap. Combine water and polenta in pan, cook, stirring, until mixture boils, simmer, covered, about 20 minutes, stirring occasionally, until mixture is thick. Remove from heat, stir in cheese, egg and butter. Spread mixture into prepared pans, refrigerate, uncovered, 1 hour.

Turn polenta onto board, cut into 8cm squares, then into triangles. Toss triangles in flour, shake away excess flour. Shallow-fry polenta in hot oil in batches until browned; drain on absorbent paper.

Serves 4.

- Recipe can be prepared 4 hours ahead.
- Storage: Covered, in refrigerator.
- Freeze: Not suitable.
- Microwave: Not suitable.

BEEF AND BAKED BEAN PIE

1 tablespoon oil
1 onion, chopped
1 (about 120g) carrot, chopped
500g minced beef
2 tablespoons tomato paste
400g can tomatoes
1 teaspoon Vegemite
1 teaspoon Worcestershire sauce
1 teaspoon dried mixed herbs
440g can baked beans in tomato sauce
⅔ cup frozen peas
440g can new potatoes, drained
30g butter, melted
¾ cup grated tasty cheese

Heat oil in pan, add onion, cook, stirring, until soft, add carrot and mince, cook, stirring, until mince is browned. Stir in paste, undrained crushed tomatoes, Vegemite, sauce and herbs. Bring to boil, simmer, uncovered, 10 minutes. Stir in beans and peas, simmer, uncovered, 5 minutes. Pour mixture into greased ovenproof dish (6 cup capacity).

Slice potatoes thinly, place over mince mixture, brush with butter, sprinkle with cheese. Bake, uncovered, in moderately hot oven about 20 minutes or until topping is crisp and browned.

Serves 4.

- Recipe can be made a day ahead.
- Storage: Covered, in refrigerator.
- Freeze: Suitable.
- Microwave: Not suitable.

Clockwise from front: Meatballs with Sour Cream and Gherkins, Beef and Beans with Polenta Triangles, Beef and Baked Bean Pie.

Plates from Mikasa Tableware.

CURRIED CHICKEN PIE

80g butter
1 onion, chopped
1 tablespoon curry powder
2 bacon rashers, chopped
2 (about 240g) carrots, sliced
2 sticks celery, sliced
300g baby mushrooms, halved
½ cup plain flour
3 teaspoons chicken stock powder
1½ cups water
¼ cup cream
30g butter, extra
750g chicken mince
1 egg, lightly beaten

PASTRY
1½ cups plain flour
125g packet cream cheese, chopped
60g butter, chopped
2 egg yolks
2 teaspoons water, approximately

Heat butter in pan, add onion and curry powder, cook, stirring, until onion is soft. Add bacon, carrots, celery and mushrooms, cook, stirring, 3 minutes. Stir in flour, stir over heat until combined. Remove from heat, gradually stir in combined stock powder, water and cream. Stir over heat until mixture boils and thickens.

Heat extra butter in pan, add mince, stir over heat until mince is changed in colour, stir into vegetable mixture; cool; refrigerate 1 hour.

Spoon mixture into 23cm pie plate. Roll pastry on floured surface large enough to cover top of dish; brush rim of plate with a little water, press on pastry top, seal and trim edges; brush with egg. Bake, uncovered, in moderately hot oven about 30 minutes or until pastry is browned.

Pastry: Sift flour into bowl, rub in cheese and butter. Add yolks and enough water to make ingredients cling together. Knead dough on floured surface until smooth, cover, refrigerate 30 minutes.

Serves 6.

■ Pie can be prepared 2 days ahead.
■ Storage: Covered, in refrigerator.
■ Freeze: Suitable.
■ Microwave: Filling suitable.

CHILLI PISTACHIO CHICKEN

1 tablespoon oil
500g minced chicken
¼ cup lime juice
1 tablespoon fish sauce
2 teaspoons chilli sauce
6 green shallots, chopped
¼ cup chopped pistachios
1 tablespoon grated fresh ginger
2 tablespoons chopped fresh
   coriander

Heat oil in pan, add mince, cook, stirring, until mince is changed in colour. Remove pan from heat, add juice and sauces; cool.

Combine mince mixture, shallots, nuts, ginger and coriander in bowl; mix well. Serve over shredded cabbage, if desired.

Serves 4.

■ Recipe best made just before serving.
■ Freeze: Not suitable.
■ Microwave: Suitable.

CHICKEN AND FIG BONBONS

⅓ cup black-eyed beans
1 cup (190g) chopped dried figs
30g butter
1 medium leek, sliced
500g minced chicken
1 teaspoon chicken stock powder
300ml carton cream
⅓ cup milk
12 sheets fillo pastry
90g butter, melted, extra

Cover beans with water in bowl, stand overnight. Drain beans, place beans in pan, cover with water, bring to boil, simmer, covered, until tender; drain. Place figs in bowl, cover with boiling water, stand 2 minutes; drain.

Heat butter in pan, add leek, cook, stirring, until soft. Add mince, cook, stirring, until mince is changed in colour. Add beans, figs, stock powder, cream and milk, stir over heat until mixture boils, simmer, uncovered, until thick; cool.

Layer 2 pastry sheets together, brushing each with extra butter. Place one sixth of mince mixture onto short end of pastry. Roll up pastry to enclose filling. Twist ends of pastry firmly to form bonbons. Repeat with remaining pastry, butter and filling. Place bonbons on greased oven trays. Bake, uncovered, in moderate oven about 20 minutes or until browned.

Serves 6.

■ Bonbons can be prepared a day
   ahead.
■ Storage: Covered, in refrigerator.
■ Freeze: Uncooked bonbons suitable.
■ Microwave: Filling suitable.

LEFT: From top: Curried Chicken Pie, Chilli Pistachio Chicken.
ABOVE: Chicken and Fig Bonbons.

BEAN AND BEEF CASSEROLE

1¼ cups (250g) dried red kidney
  beans
750g minced beef
1½ cups (110g) stale breadcrumbs
1 egg, lightly beaten
½ teaspoon ground nutmeg
½ teaspoon ground allspice
2 tablespoons olive oil
1 onion, chopped
2 cloves garlic, crushed
2 (about 240g) carrots, sliced
2 sticks celery, sliced
2 small beef stock cubes
2 cups water
1 cinnamon stick

2 small fresh red chillies
1 teaspoon plain flour
2 teaspoons water, extra
¼ cup chopped fresh flat-leaf parsley

Cover beans in bowl with water; stand overnight. Drain beans, place in pan, cover with water, bring to boil, simmer, covered, about 15 minutes or until beans are just tender; drain.

Combine mince, breadcrumbs, egg and spices in bowl; mix well. Shape level tablespoons of mixture into balls. Heat half the oil in pan, add meatballs, cook, stirring, until well browned; drain on absorbent paper.

Heat remaining oil in pan, add onion,

garlic, carrots and celery, cook, stirring, until onion is soft. Return meatballs to pan, stir in crumbled stock cubes, water, cinnamon stick and chillies. Bring to boil, simmer, covered, 10 minutes. Add beans, simmer, covered, further 10 minutes or until beans are tender. Stir in flour blended with extra water, stir over heat until mixture boils and thickens. Discard cinnamon stick and chillies, stir in parsley.

Serves 6.

▥ Recipe can be made a day ahead.
▥ Storage: Covered, in refrigerator.
▥ Freeze: Suitable.
▥ Microwave: Not suitable.

CAPPELLACCI WITH MUSHROOM SAUCE

Use 60g eggs in this recipe.
2 cups plain flour
⅓ cup olive oil
2 tablespoons water
2 eggs
1 egg, lightly beaten, extra

FILLING
2 tablespoons olive oil
150g minced beef
½ cup roasted hazelnuts, finely
**   chopped**
2 tablespoons grated parmesan
**   cheese**
2 tablespoons chopped fresh parsley
2 tablespoons chopped fresh chives
½ teaspoon ground nutmeg
¼ cup cream

MUSHROOM SAUCE
30g butter
250g mushrooms, sliced
1 clove garlic, crushed
1 cup dry white wine
1 cup cream
1 cup water
2 tablespoons chopped fresh parsley

Combine flour, oil, water and eggs in food processor. Process ingredients until mixture forms a ball. Knead dough on lightly floured surface until smooth.

Cut dough in half, roll each half through pasta machine on thickest setting. Fold dough in half, roll through machine. Repeat folding and rolling several times until dough is smooth and elastic, dusting dough with a little extra flour when necessary. Adjust setting to become thinner with each roll.

Roll dough until 2mm thick; cut into 9cm rounds. Brush rounds with a little extra egg; place level teaspoon of filling in the centre of each round. Fold rounds in half, press edges together to seal. Brush corners with water, pinch points together.

Add cappellacci to large pan of boiling water, boil, uncovered, about 8 minutes or until just tender; drain. Serve cappellacci with mushroom sauce.
Filling: Heat oil in pan, add mince, cook, stirring, until browned; remove from heat, cool. Combine mince with remaining ingredients in bowl; mix well.
Mushroom Sauce: Heat butter in pan, add mushrooms and garlic, cook, stirring, 3 minutes. Add wine, bring to boil, simmer, uncovered, until wine is reduced by one third. Stir in cream and water, simmer, uncovered, until sauce is thick; stir in parsley.

Serves 4.

- Cappellacci and sauce can be prepared a day ahead.
- Storage: Covered, in refrigerator.
- Freeze: Uncooked cappellacci suitable.
- Microwave: Not suitable.

SHEPHERD'S PIE WITH KUMARA TOPPING

1 tablespoon oil
1 onion, chopped
750g minced chicken
⅔ cup water
1 teaspoon chicken stock powder
⅓ cup dry white wine
1 teaspoon dried mixed herbs
2 tablespoons tomato paste
¾ cup frozen peas
¾ cup frozen corn kernels
1½ tablespoons cornflour
2 tablespoons water, extra

TOPPING
3 large (about 600g) potatoes,
**   chopped**
400g kumara, chopped
¼ cup cream
40g butter

Heat oil in pan, add onion, cook, stirring, until soft, add mince, cook, stirring, until mince is changed in colour. Stir in water, stock powder, wine, herbs, paste, peas and corn. Bring to boil, simmer, uncovered, about 5 minutes or until vegetables are tender. Stir in blended cornflour and extra water, stir over heat until mixture boils and thickens.

Spoon mixture into greased (5 cup capacity) ovenproof dish. Pipe topping over mince mixture, bake, uncovered, in moderate oven about 30 minutes or until topping is lightly browned and pie is heated through.
Topping: Boil, steam or microwave potatoes and kumara until tender; drain. Place in bowl, mash with cream and butter until smooth.

Serves 4 to 6.

- Recipe can be made a day ahead.
- Storage: Covered, in refrigerator.
- Freeze: Suitable.
- Microwave: Potatoes and kumara suitable.

LEFT: From top: Bean and Beef Casserole, Cappellacci with Mushroom Sauce.
ABOVE: Shepherd's Pie with Kumara Topping.

Left: Plate from Mikasa Tableware.

COCONUT CHICKEN CURRY WITH PILAF

1 tablespoon oil
1 onion, chopped
1 clove garlic, crushed
1 tablespoon curry powder
500g minced chicken
225g can coconut milk
300g can Tomato Supreme

PILAF
2 tablespoons oil
1 onion, chopped
1 green pepper, chopped
1 red pepper, chopped
2 cups long grain rice
1 teaspoon chicken stock powder
1 litre (4 cups) water
½ cup frozen peas, thawed
2 green shallots, chopped

Heat oil in pan, add onion and garlic, cook, stirring, until onion is soft. Add curry powder, stir over heat 1 minute. Add mince, stir over heat until mince is changed in colour, add milk and Tomato Supreme. Bring to boil, simmer, uncovered, about 20 minutes or until mixture is thickened. Serve with pilaf.

Pilaf: Heat oil in pan, add onion and peppers, cook, stirring, until onion is soft; add rice, stock powder and water. Bring to boil, simmer, covered, about 15 minutes or until liquid is evaporated and rice is tender. Stir in peas and shallots, stir until heated through.

Serves 4.

■ Curry can be made a day ahead.
■ Storage: Covered, in refrigerator.
■ Freeze: Pilaf suitable.
■ Microwave: Not suitable.

CHICKEN LASAGNE

30g butter
1 red Spanish onion, chopped
2 cloves garlic, crushed
500g minced chicken
½ teaspoon dried rosemary leaves
¼ teaspoon dried thyme leaves
2 tomatoes, peeled, chopped
200g chopped frozen spinach, thawed, drained
6 lasagne pasta sheets
1 tablespoon grated parmesan cheese
1 tablespoon packaged breadcrumbs
¼ teaspoon ground nutmeg

CHEESE SAUCE
50g butter
⅓ cup plain flour
2 cups milk
1 cup (125g) grated tasty cheese

Heat butter in pan, add onion and garlic, cook, stirring, until onion is soft, add mince, cook, stirring, until mince is changed in colour. Stir in herbs, tomatoes and spinach, cook, stirring, until most of the liquid is evaporated.

Add pasta to pan of boiling water, boil, uncovered until just tender; drain.

Line base of greased 16cm x 25cm ovenproof dish with 3 pasta sheets, top with half the mince mixture and half the cheese sauce. Cover with remaining pasta sheets, top with remaining mince mixture and remaining cheese sauce. Sprinkle with combined cheese, breadcrumbs and nutmeg. Bake, uncovered, in moderate oven about 30 minutes or until browned.

Cheese Sauce: Melt butter in pan, stir in flour, cook, stirring, until dry and grainy, remove from heat. Gradually stir in milk, stir over heat until sauce boils and thickens. Remove from heat, stir in cheese.

Serves 6.

■ Recipe can be made a day ahead
■ Storage: Covered, in refrigerator.
■ Freeze: Suitable.
■ Microwave: Pasta suitable.

PASTA CAKE WITH MEATBALLS

500g minced beef
1 clove garlic, crushed
2 tablespoons chopped fresh parsley
2 tablespoons grated parmesan cheese
1 egg, lightly beaten
2 tablespoons tomato paste
½ cup stale breadcrumbs
plain flour
oil for shallow-frying
500g penne pasta
⅓ cup milk
2 tablespoons grated tasty cheese
2 tablespoons grated parmesan cheese, extra

SAUCE
90g butter
¼ cup plain flour
3 cups milk
**2 tablespoons grated parmesan
    cheese**
¼ teaspoon ground nutmeg

Line 25cm springform tin with foil, grease foil lightly.

Combine mince, garlic, parsley, cheese, egg, paste and breadcrumbs in bowl; mix well. Roll 2 level teaspoons of mixture into balls. Toss meatballs in flour, shake away excess flour. Shallow-fry meatballs in hot oil in batches until well browned; drain on absorbent paper.

Add pasta to large pan of boiling water, boil, uncovered, until just tender; drain. Combine two-thirds of sauce in bowl with meatballs and pasta. Spread pasta mixture into prepared tin, pour milk over mixture, spread with remaining sauce, sprinkle with combined tasty cheese and extra parmesan cheese.

Bake, uncovered, in moderately hot oven about 30 minutes or until browned. Stand pasta cake 15 minutes before removing from tin.

Sauce: Melt butter in pan, add flour, stir over heat until bubbling. Remove pan from heat, gradually stir in milk, stir over heat until sauce boils and thickens. Stir in cheese and nutmeg.

Serves 6.

- Recipe can be made a day ahead.
- Storage: Covered, in refrigerator.
- Freeze: Suitable.
- Microwave: Pasta suitable.

CURRIED MINCE ROLL IN CORNBREAD

⅔ cup polenta
1 cup self-raising flour
½ cup plain flour
½ red pepper, finely chopped
½ green pepper, finely chopped
1 tablespoon sugar
½ cup water
2 eggs, lightly beaten

CURRIED MINCE ROLL
1 tablespoon oil
1 red Spanish onion, finely chopped
2 cloves garlic, crushed
3 teaspoons curry powder
2 teaspoons paprika
1 teaspoon sambal oelek
1 teaspoon ground cumin
400g minced beef
1 cup (70g) stale breadcrumbs

PEPPER SALAD
½ red pepper
½ green pepper
1 green shallot
2 tablespoons olive oil
2 tablespoons white vinegar
½ teaspoon sugar
½ teaspoon sambal oelek

Combine polenta, sifted flours, peppers and sugar in bowl, stir in combined water and eggs. Spread half polenta mixture into greased 14cm x 21cm loaf pan. Place curried mince roll in centre of mixture. Spread remaining polenta mixture over top and sides of roll. Bake, uncovered, in moderate oven about 40 minutes or until browned and cooked through. Stand loaf in pan 5 minutes before turning from pan; cool. Serve with pepper salad.

Curried Mince Roll: Heat oil in pan, add onion, garlic, curry powder, paprika, sambal oelek and cumin, stir over heat until fragrant. Process onion mixture, mince and breadcrumbs until combined. Spoon mixture onto piece of foil, roll into sausage shape about 20cm long. Wrap roll in foil, twist ends firmly to seal. Cook in pan of simmering water about 20 minutes or until firm, remove from water; cool.

Pepper Salad: Cut peppers and shallot into thin strips, combine with remaining ingredients in bowl; mix well.

Serves 6 to 8

- Recipe can be made a day ahead.
- Storage: Covered, in refrigerator.
- Freeze: Cooked loaf suitable.
- Microwave: Curried mince roll suitable.

LEFT: From top: Coconut Chicken Curry with Pilaf, Chicken Lasagne.
ABOVE: From top: Curried Mince Roll in Cornbread, Pasta Cake with Meatballs.

LENTIL AND BEEF STEW

2 tablespoons oil
2 onions, chopped
500g minced beef
2 (about 240g) carrots, chopped
2 sticks celery, chopped
400g can tomatoes
2 small beef stock cubes
1 cup water
1 cup (200g) red lentils, rinsed,
    drained
¼ cup dry red wine
1½ cups water, extra
2 tablespoons tomato paste
2 teaspoons sugar
¼ cup shredded fresh basil

Heat oil in pan, add onions and mince, cook, stirring, until mince is browned. Stir in carrots, celery, undrained crushed tomatoes, crumbled stock cubes and water. Bring to boil, simmer, covered, about 30 minutes or until vegetables are tender. Stir in lentils, wine, extra water, paste and sugar. Bring to boil, simmer, uncovered, until lentils are tender and mixture is thick. Stir in basil.

Serves 6.
- Recipe can be made a day ahead.
- Storage: Covered, in refrigerator.
- Freeze: Suitable.
- Microwave: Not suitable.

BEEF AND CHOPPED EGG IN FILLO PASTRY

6 sheets fillo pastry
60g butter, melted
3 hard-boiled eggs, chopped
½ cup grated parmesan cheese
½ cup grated tasty cheese

FILLING
2 teaspoons oil
1 red Spanish onion, chopped
1 clove garlic, crushed
500g minced beef
1 red pepper, chopped
¼ cup sun-dried tomatoes, sliced
1 teaspoon beef stock powder
¼ cup water
¼ cup tomato paste
2 tablespoons chopped fresh parsley
½ teaspoon seasoned pepper

Brush 1 pastry sheet with butter, lay next sheet crossways over first sheet, brush with butter; repeat brushing and crossways layering with remaining butter and sheets. Lift pastry sheets into greased 23cm pie plate, leave pastry overhanging side.

Spoon filling into pastry, sprinkle with eggs, then combined cheeses. Fold overhanging edges of pastry to centre of pie, brushing pastry with remaining butter. Bake, uncovered, in moderate oven about 35 minutes or until lightly browned.

Filling: Heat oil in pan, add onion and garlic, cook, stirring, until onion is soft. Add mince, cook, stirring, until browned. Stir in remaining ingredients, cook, uncovered, until mixture is thick.

Serves 6.
- Recipe can be made a day ahead.
- Storage: Covered, in refrigerator.
- Freeze: Cooked pie suitable.
- Microwave: Not suitable.

BEEF SAUSAGE WITH ONION GRAVY

500g minced beef
4 bacon rashers, chopped
1 onion, chopped
1 cup (70g) stale breadcrumbs
1 tablespoon Worcestershire sauce
1 tablespoon tomato sauce
1 teaspoon grated lemon rind
2 eggs

GRAVY
60g butter
2 large (about 400g) onions, sliced
1½ tablespoons plain flour
2 cups water
2 teaspoons beef stock powder
¼ cup dry red wine
2 teaspoons Worcestershire sauce
1 teaspoon sugar
1 teaspoon French mustard

Process all ingredients until well combined. Place mince mixture on piece of lightly floured calico. Using wet hands, mould mixture into 30cm sausage; roll calico around sausage, tie ends of roll securely with string.

Place sausage in large pan of simmering water, simmer, covered, about 2 hours or until sausage is firm. Drain sausage; stand 10 minutes before slicing. Serve sausage with gravy.

Gravy: Heat butter in pan, add onions, cook, stirring, until soft. Stir in flour, stir over heat until flour is lightly browned. Remove from heat, gradually stir in combined water, stock powder, wine, sauce, sugar and mustard, stir over heat until mixture boils and thickens.

Serves 6.
- Sausage best made close to serving.
- Freeze: Suitable.
- Microwave: Gravy suitable.

Clockwise from back: Lentil and Beef Stew, Beef and Chopped Egg in Fillo Pastry, Beef Sausage with Onion Gravy.

SPICY CORNMEAL CREPES

1 cup (200g) cornmeal
2 cups plain flour
2 eggs, lightly beaten
2¾ cups water
1 cup (125g) grated tasty cheese
½ cup sour cream

FILLING
1 tablespoon oil
1 clove garlic, crushed
1 onion, chopped
1 green pepper, chopped
500g minced beef
410g can tomatoes

SAUCE
1 tablespoon oil
1 onion, chopped
¼ teaspoon chilli powder
⅔ cup tomato puree
⅓ cup water

Combine cornmeal and sifted flour in bowl; stir in combined eggs and water gradually; beat until smooth (or blend or process all ingredients until smooth).

Pour 2 to 3 tablespoons of batter into heated greased heavy-based pan; cook until browned underneath. Turn, brown other side. Repeat with remaining batter. You need 16 crepes for this recipe.

Divide filling evenly between crepes; roll up to a parcel shape to enclose filling. Place parcels in single layer seam side down in large, shallow, greased ovenproof dish.

Pour over sauce; top with cheese. Bake, uncovered, in moderate oven about 30 minutes or until crepes and filling are heated through. Serve crepes topped with sour cream.

Filling: Heat oil in pan, add garlic, onion and pepper, cook, stirring, until onion is soft. Add mince, stir over heat until browned, stir in undrained crushed tomatoes. Bring to boil, simmer, uncovered, about 10 minutes or until liquid is evaporated and mixture is thick.

Sauce: Heat oil in pan, add onion and chilli powder, cook, stirring, until onion is soft. Stir in puree and water; bring to boil, simmer, uncovered, about 2 minutes or until slightly thickened.

Serves 4 to 6.

- ■ Crepes, filling and sauce can be made separately a day ahead.
- ■ Storage: Covered, in refrigerator.
- ■ Freeze: Suitable.
- ■ Microwave: Sauce suitable.

BEAN SALAD IN BEEF AND ONION SHELLS

250g minced beef
1 small onion, chopped
35g packet taco seasoning mix
½ cup wholemeal plain flour
¼ cup white plain flour
1 tablespoon water, approximately
2 tablespoons oil

BEAN SALAD
310g can red kidney beans, rinsed, drained
1 large (about 250g) tomato, seeded, chopped
½ cup corn kernels
2 green shallots, chopped
2 sticks celery, chopped
¼ cup oil
2 tablespoons lemon juice
pinch chilli powder
1 tablespoon chopped fresh chives

Combine mince, onion, seasoning mix and flours in large bowl, mix well, stir in enough water to form a stiff mixture. Knead mixture on lightly floured surface until smooth. Divide mixture into 4 portions, roll each portion into a 20cm round.

Heat oil in pan, cook mince rounds on both sides until lightly browned. Press each round over a 6cm-high ovenproof cup on oven tray. Bake shells in moderate oven for about 10 minutes or until well browned; cool. Fill shells with bean salad just before serving.

Bean Salad: Combine all ingredients in bowl; mix well.

Serves 2 to 4.

- ■ Recipe can be prepared 6 hours ahead.
- ■ Storage: Covered, in refrigerator.
- ■ Freeze: Not suitable.
- ■ Microwave: Not suitable.

LEFT: From back: Bean Salad in Beef and Onion Shells, Spicy Cornmeal Crepes. ABOVE: Sausage Apple Roll.

Left: Pottery from Something Special Gallery.

SAUSAGE APPLE ROLL

2 cups self-raising flour
30g butter
2 teaspoons seasoned pepper
⅔ cup milk, approximately

FILLING
1 large (about 200g) apple, peeled, grated
1 large (200g) onion, grated
500g minced pork and veal
½ cup stale breadcrumbs
1 tablespoon plain flour
1 teaspoon sambal oelek
1 tablespoon curry powder
1 tablespoon chopped fresh coriander
2 tablespoons chopped fresh parsley

Sift flour into bowl, rub in butter. Stir in pepper and enough milk to mix to a soft dough. Knead gently on lightly floured surface until smooth. Roll dough out to a 20cm x 36cm rectangle. Place filling lengthways on dough, leaving a 3cm border at either end. Brush edges with a little more milk. Fold dough over to enclose filling, seal ends with fork.

Place roll seam side down on lightly greased oven tray, cut slits in top of roll, brush with a little more milk. Bake in moderately hot oven about 20 minutes, reduce heat to moderate, bake further 30 minutes or until roll is browned. Stand roll 10 minutes before slicing.

Filling: Squeeze excess liquid from apple and onion; combine in bowl with remaining ingredients; mix well.

Serves 4.

- ■ Recipe can be made a day ahead.
- ■ Storage: Covered, in refrigerator.
- ■ Freeze: Suitable.
- ■ Microwave: Not suitable.

CHICKEN AND ASPARAGUS CREPES

1 cup (125g) grated tasty cheese
½ teaspoon paprika

CREPES
1 cup plain flour
3 eggs, lightly beaten
1 tablespoon oil
1¼ cups milk

FILLING
1 tablespoon oil
2 leeks, sliced
500g minced chicken
1 bunch (12 spears) fresh asparagus, chopped
300ml carton thickened cream
1 tablespoon seeded mustard
2 small chicken stock cubes
⅔ cup water
2 tablespoons cornflour
½ cup dry white wine
2 tablespoons chopped fresh chives

Divide filling between crepes, fold crepes, place in single layer in large shallow flameproof dish, sprinkle with cheese and paprika. Grill until cheese is melted.
Crepes: Sift flour into bowl; gradually stir in combined eggs, oil and milk, beat until smooth (or, blend or process all ingredients until smooth). Pour 2 to 3 tablespoons of batter into heated greased heavy-based pan; cook until lightly browned underneath. Turn crepe, brown other side. Repeat with remaining batter. You will need 12 crepes for this recipe.
Filling: Heat oil in pan, add leeks, cook, stirring, until soft. Stir in mince and asparagus, cook, stirring, until mince is changed in colour. Stir in cream, mustard, crumbled stock cubes, water, and blended cornflour and wine, stir over heat until mixture boils and thickens; stir in chives, mix well.

Serves 4 to 6.

- Crepes and filling can be made a day ahead.
- Storage: Covered, in refrigerator.
- Freeze: Crepes suitable.
- Microwave: Filling suitable.

BOLOGNAISE POTATOES

4 large (about 800g) potatoes
⅓ cup grated tasty cheese
¼ cup grated fresh parmesan cheese

FILLING
1 tablespoon olive oil
1 onion, chopped
1 clove garlic, crushed
400g minced beef
410g can tomatoes
2 tablespoons tomato paste
1 small beef stock cube
1 tablespoon chopped fresh basil

Boil, steam or microwave potatoes until tender. Cut in half, scoop out flesh leaving 1cm shell. Mash flesh, combine with filling; spoon into shells. Place on oven tray, sprinkle with cheeses; grill until melted.
Filling: Heat oil in pan, add onion and garlic, cook, stirring, until onion is soft. Add mince, stir over heat until mince is well browned. Add undrained crushed tomatoes and remaining ingredients; bring to boil, simmer, uncovered, about 5 minutes or until mixture thickens slightly.

Serves 4.

- Recipe can be made a day ahead.
- Storage: Covered, in refrigerator.
- Freeze: Not suitable.
- Microwave: Potatoes suitable.

BEEF AND NOODLE OMELETTE

1 teaspoon sesame oil
1 onion, finely chopped
400g minced beef
2 tablespoons chopped fresh coriander
100g dried egg noodles
6 eggs, lightly beaten
1 tablespoon oil

GINGER SAUCE
2 teaspoons cornflour
1 cup water
1 tablespoon white vinegar
2 teaspoons light soy sauce
1 tablespoon sugar
2 teaspoons grated fresh ginger
½ red pepper, thinly sliced
2 green shallots, thinly sliced

Heat sesame oil in pan, add onion and mince, stir over heat until mince is well browned; stir in coriander. Add noodles to pan of boiling water, boil, uncovered, until tender, drain, rinse under cold water; drain well. Chop noodles roughly.

Combine mince mixture, noodles and eggs in large bowl; mix well. Heat oil in large pan, pour in egg mixture, cook until omelette is browned underneath. Place pan under hot grill, cook until top is set and browned. Serve with ginger sauce.

Ginger Sauce: Blend cornflour with a little of the water in pan, stir in remaining water, vinegar, sauce and sugar, stir over heat until sauce boils and thickens. Stir in ginger, pepper and shallots.

Serves 4.

■ Recipe best made just before serving.
■ Freeze: Not suitable.
■ Microwave: Ginger sauce suitable.

LEFT: Chicken and Asparagus Crepes.
ABOVE: From top: Bolognaise Potatoes, Beef and Noodle Omelette.

BARBECUE BONUS

We've cooked up some great little sizzlers in tasty burgers, patties, meatballs, kebabs and homemade sausages to serve with tempting sauces and interesting butters. But we've explored more! Think of pizza with a minced beef base and cheesy bacon topping, or our curry scone rolls, very moreish with mint butter. On the whole, we've mostly used a barbecue plate in this section, but results will be equally good if you grill or fry as individual recipes suggest. As with all the recipes in this book, fine mince is best, and will help you to achieve results like ours.

PIZZA TOPPED BURGERS

750g minced beef
1 onion, chopped
1 clove garlic, crushed
1 egg, lightly beaten
grated fresh parmesan cheese

PIZZA TOPPING
2 tablespoons olive oil
1 onion, chopped
1 clove garlic, crushed
1 red pepper, chopped
200g baby mushrooms, sliced
400g can tomatoes
1 teaspoon sugar
2 tablespoons chopped fresh basil

Combine mince, onion, garlic and egg in bowl; mix well. Shape mixture into 8 patties. Barbecue or grill burgers until browned and cooked through. Serve with topping, sprinkle with cheese.
Topping: Heat oil in pan, add onion, garlic and pepper, cook, stirring, until onion is soft. Add mushrooms, cook, stirring, until mushrooms are tender. Stir in undrained crushed tomatoes and sugar. Bring to boil, simmer, uncovered, about 10 minutes or until sauce is thick, stir in basil.
Serves 4 to 6.

■ Patties can be prepared a day ahead.
■ Storage: Covered, in refrigerator.
■ Freeze: Uncooked patties suitable.
■ Microwave: Not suitable.

Pizza Topped Burgers.

Combine mince, onion, paprika, oregano, garlic and sauce in bowl; mix well. Press mixture into 28cm pizza pan. Spread with paste, top with bacon, mozzarella cheese, mushrooms, pepper and tomato, sprinkle with parmesan cheese and basil. Cover pizza with foil, barbecue 10 minutes, remove foil, drain off juices, barbecue, uncovered, until mince is cooked through and cheese melted, drain off juices; serve hot.

Serves 4 to 6.

- Recipe best made just before serving.
- Freeze: Not suitable.
- Microwave: Not suitable.

BARBECUED MEATBALLS WITH EGGPLANT PUREE

1kg minced beef
1 onion, chopped
2 cloves garlic, crushed
½ teaspoon ground cinnamon
1 teaspoon ground allspice
⅓ cup pine nuts, chopped
⅓ cup chopped raisins
1½ cups (110g) stale breadcrumbs
1 egg, lightly beaten
2 tablespoons olive oil

EGGPLANT PUREE
1 small (about 250g) eggplant
coarse cooking salt
¼ cup olive oil
2 cloves garlic, crushed
2 tablespoons lemon juice
2 tablespoons plain yogurt
1 tablespoon chopped fresh mint

Combine mince, onion, garlic, spices, nuts, raisins, breadcrumbs and egg in bowl; mix well. Shape level tablespoons of mixture into balls. Heat oil on barbecue plate or in pan, add meatballs, cook until browned and tender. Serve hot with warm eggplant puree.

Eggplant Puree: Peel and chop eggplant, sprinkle with salt; stand 30 minutes. Rinse eggplant under cold water, drain on absorbent paper. Heat oil in pan, add eggplant and garlic, cook, stirring, about 2 minutes or until eggplant is soft. Blend or process eggplant until smooth, stir in juice, yogurt and mint.

Serves 6.

- Meatballs can be prepared a day ahead.
- Storage: Covered, in refrigerator.
- Freeze: Meatballs suitable.
- Microwave: Not suitable.

BEETROOT BURGERS

500g minced beef
1 onion, grated
1 teaspoon seeded mustard
½ cup packaged breadcrumbs
1 tablespoon chopped fresh basil
1 medium (about 150g) beetroot, peeled, grated
1 egg, lightly beaten
2 tablespoons oil
6 hamburger buns
6 lettuce leaves
1 large tomato, sliced
6 pineapple rings

Combine mince, onion, mustard, breadcrumbs, basil, beetroot and egg in bowl; mix well. Shape mixture into 6 patties.

Heat oil on barbecue plate or in pan, cook patties until browned and cooked through; drain on absorbent paper. Split buns in half, toast buns; fill with lettuce, tomato, patties and pineapple.

Serves 4 to 6.

- Patties can be prepared a day ahead.
- Storage: Covered, in refrigerator.
- Freeze: Uncooked patties suitable.
- Microwave: Not suitable.

BARBECUED MINCE PIZZA

3 bacon rashers, chopped
500g minced beef
1 large onion, chopped
½ teaspoon paprika
½ teaspoon dried oregano leaves
2 cloves garlic, crushed
2 tablespoons sweet chilli sauce
¼ cup tomato paste
250g mozzarella cheese, sliced
90g mushrooms, sliced
1 small green pepper, sliced
1 medium tomato, sliced
2 tablespoons grated parmesan cheese
½ teaspoon dried basil leaves

Add bacon to pan, cook, stirring, until crisp; drain on absorbent paper.

CHEESY POTATO SHELLS WITH ONIONS

6 large (about 1.2kg) potatoes
1 cup (125g) grated tasty cheese
1 tablespoon oil
2 large onions, sliced

FILLING
2 teaspoons oil
1 onion, chopped
1 clove garlic, crushed
400g minced beef
130g mushrooms, sliced
½ cup water
1 teaspoon beef stock powder
2 teaspoons seeded mustard
1 tablespoon chopped fresh parsley

TOPPING
40g butter
2 tablespoons plain flour
1 cup milk
1 cup (125g) grated tasty cheese

Wrap potatoes in foil, cook in barbecue coals (or hot oven) about 1 hour or until potatoes are tender.

Cut tops from potatoes, scoop out flesh leaving a 1cm shell. Reserve ½ cup flesh for the filling, use remaining flesh for another purpose.

Spoon filling into potatoes, press in firmly. Place potatoes on oven tray, spoon topping over filling, sprinkle with cheese. Bake potatoes, uncovered, in moderate oven about 20 minutes or until browned and heated through.

Heat oil on barbecue plate or in pan, add onions, cook, stirring, until browned. Serve potatoes with onions.

Filling: Heat oil in pan, add onion and garlic, cook, stirring, until onion is soft. Add mince, cook, stirring, until browned. Stir in reserved potato flesh, mushrooms, water, stock powder, mustard and parsley. Stir over heat until combined.

Topping: Melt butter in pan, stir in flour, stir over heat until bubbling. Remove from heat, gradually stir in milk, stir over heat until sauce boils and thickens. Remove from heat, stir in cheese.

Serves 6.

■ Recipe best made just before serving.
■ Freeze: Not suitable.
■ Microwave: Topping suitable.

BEEF KEBABS WITH FRUITY RELISH

450g can crushed pineapple in heavy syrup
500g minced beef
½ cup coconut
½ cup stale breadcrumbs
1 egg, lightly beaten
1 teaspoon turmeric
2 teaspoons ground cumin
2 teaspoons ground coriander
1 teaspoon curry powder

FRUITY RELISH
¼ cup shredded coconut
1 banana, chopped
425g can peach halves in syrup, drained, chopped
2 tablespoons lime juice
1 tablespoon chopped fresh mint

Place 2 tablespoons of drained pineapple in large bowl. Reserve remaining syrup and pineapple. Add mince, coconut, breadcrumbs, egg and spices to bowl; mix well. Shape level tablespoons of mixture into sausages about 4cm long. Thread onto 12 skewers; grill or barbecue until cooked through. Serve with fruity relish.
Fruity Relish: Combine reserved pineapple and syrup with remaining ingredients in bowl; mix well, cover, refrigerate several hours or overnight.

Serves 4 to 6.

■ Recipe can be prepared a day ahead.
■ Storage: Covered, in refrigerator.
■ Freeze: Not suitable.
■ Microwave: Not suitable.

PEPPERED PATTIES WITH BRANDY SAUCE

1kg minced beef
3 green shallots, chopped
2 small beef stock cubes
1 small red pepper, finely chopped
2 tablespoons cracked black peppercorns
1 tablespoon oil

BRANDY SAUCE
60g butter
2 tablespoons brandy
300ml carton cream
¼ cup chopped fresh parsley

Combine mince, shallots, crumbled stock cubes and pepper in bowl; mix well. Shape mixture into 8 patties. Roll each patty in peppercorns. Heat oil on barbecue plate or in pan, add patties, cook until tender. Serve with brandy sauce.
Brandy Sauce: Heat butter in pan, add brandy and cream, bring to boil, simmer, uncovered, about 3 minutes or until sauce is slightly thickened; stir in parsley.

Serves 6 to 8.

■ Patties can be prepared a day ahead.
■ Storage: Covered, in refrigerator.
■ Freeze: Uncooked patties suitable.
■ Microwave: Sauce suitable.

CHICKEN AND BACON BURGERS WITH AVOCADO

1kg minced chicken
1 onion, chopped
2 cloves garlic, crushed
1 teaspoon seasoned pepper
1 teaspoon chicken stock powder
2½ cups (175g) stale breadcrumbs
1 egg, lightly beaten
4 bacon rashers
1 tablespoon oil

AVOCADO TOPPING
2 small avocados
1 (about 130g) tomato, peeled, chopped
½ red Spanish onion, chopped
1 tablespoon chilli sauce

Combine mince, onion, garlic, pepper, stock powder, breadcrumbs and egg in bowl; mix well. Shape mixture into 8 patties. Cut bacon in half lengthways, wrap around patties, secure with toothpicks. Heat oil on barbecue plate or in pan, add burgers, cook until browned and tender. Serve with avocado topping.

Avocado Topping: Blend or process avocados until smooth; transfer to bowl, stir in remaining ingredients.

Serves 6 to 8.

■ Burgers can be prepared a day ahead.
■ Storage: Covered, in refrigerator.
■ Freeze: Uncooked burgers suitable.
■ Microwave: Not suitable.

LEFT: From top: Peppered Patties with Brandy Sauce, Beef Kebabs with Fruity Relish.
BELOW: Chicken and Bacon Burgers with Avocado.

Left: Plates from Amy's Tableware.

HOMEMADE BEEF SAUSAGES

1 tablespoon oil
1 onion, finely chopped
1kg minced beef
500g sausage mince
1 cup (70g) stale breadcrumbs
1 teaspoon dried mixed herbs
3 small beef stock cubes
⅔ cup water

Heat oil in pan, add onion, cook, stirring, until soft. Combine onion mixture, minces, breadcrumbs, herbs, crumbled stock cubes and water in bowl; mix well. Divide mixture into 16 portions. Place each portion onto a piece of plastic wrap, roll into thick sausage shapes. Wrap each roll in foil, twist ends firmly to seal. Poach rolls in pan of simmering water about 10 minutes or until sausages are cooked through. Remove rolls from water; stand 10 minutes. Remove plastic wrap and foil. Cook sausages on oiled barbecue plate or in pan until browned.

Serves 6 to 8.

- Sausages can be made 3 days ahead.
- Storage: Covered, in refrigerator.
- Freeze: Uncooked sausages suitable.
- Microwave: Not suitable.

116

BURGERS WITH GUACAMOLE AND CABBAGE SALAD

700g minced beef
1 clove garlic, crushed
1 egg
½ cup stale breadcrumbs
pinch of ground cumin
pinch chilli powder
4 green shallots, chopped

GUACAMOLE
1 avocado
¼ cup lemon juice
1 clove garlic, crushed

CABBAGE SALAD
2 tablespoons tarragon wine vinegar
¾ cup olive oil
½ teaspoon sugar
1 teaspoon seeded mustard
1 clove garlic, crushed
4 green shallots, chopped
2½ cups (about 200g) finely shredded white cabbage

Combine all ingredients in bowl; mix well. Shape mixture into 8 burgers. Barbecue or grill burgers until browned and cooked through. Serve with guacamole and cabbage salad.
Guacamole: Blend or process all ingredients until smooth.

Cabbage Salad: Combine vinegar, oil, sugar, mustard, garlic and shallots in jar; shake well. Pour dressing over cabbage in bowl; cover, stand 1 hour.

Serves 6 to 8.
- Recipe can be prepared 3 hours ahead.
- Storage: Covered, in refrigerator.
- Freeze: Uncooked burgers suitable.
- Microwave: Not suitable.

LAMB KOFTA WITH HUMMUS AND GRILLED PEPPERS

500g minced lamb
1 small onion, chopped
1 clove garlic, crushed
¼ cup chopped fresh coriander
1 teaspoon paprika
1 teaspoon ground cumin
1 teaspoon ground cinnamon
pinch cayenne pepper
1 tablespoon oil

HUMMUS
2 teaspoons oil
310g can chick peas, rinsed, drained
⅔ cup tahini paste
3 teaspoons sesame oil
2 cloves garlic, crushed
¾ cup lemon juice
1 tablespoon water

GRILLED PEPPERS
1 red pepper
1 green pepper
1 yellow pepper

Combine mince, onion, garlic, coriander and spices in bowl; mix well. Divide mixture into 8 portions. Shape mixture onto skewers using wet hands; refrigerate 1 hour. Heat oil on barbecue plate or in pan, cook kofta until well browned and cooked through. Serve kofta with hummus and grilled peppers.
Hummus: Blend or process all ingredients until smooth.
Grilled Peppers: Quarter peppers; remove seeds and membrane. Grill peppers, skin side up, until skin blisters and blackens. Peel skin, slice peppers.

Serves 4 to 6.
- Recipe can be prepared a day ahead.
- Storage: Covered, in refrigerator.
- Freeze: Uncooked kofta suitable.
- Microwave: Not suitable.

LEFT: From left: Burgers with Guacamole and Cabbage Salad, Homemade Beef Sausages.
BELOW: Lamb Kofta with Hummus and Grilled Peppers.

BURGERS WITH ASSORTED BUTTERS

1kg minced beef
1 onion, chopped
2 cloves garlic, crushed
2 teaspoons beef stock powder
1 egg, lightly beaten
1½ cups (110g) stale breadcrumbs
2 tablespoons oil

ANCHOVY BUTTER
125g butter, softened
45g can anchovy fillets, drained, chopped
2 tablespoons chopped fresh basil
1 clove garlic, crushed

MUSTARD BUTTER
125g butter, softened
2 tablespoons seeded mustard
2 tablespoons chopped fresh chives
1 teaspoon grated lemon rind

CORIANDER CURRY BUTTER
1 teaspoon curry powder
1 teaspoon ground cumin
1 clove garlic, crushed
125g butter, softened
1 tablespoon chopped fresh coriander

TOMATO OLIVE BUTTER
125g butter, softened
2 tablespoons tomato paste
1½ tablespoons chopped black olives
1 clove garlic, crushed
¼ cup grated fresh parmesan cheese

Combine mince, onion, garlic, stock powder, egg and breadcrumbs in bowl; mix well. Shape mixture into 12 burgers. Heat oil on barbecue plate or in pan, add burgers, cook until well browned and tender. Serve with butters.

Anchovy Butter: Combine all ingredients in bowl; mix well.

Mustard Butter: Combine all ingredients in bowl; mix well.

Coriander Curry Butter: Combine curry powder, cumin and garlic in pan, stir over heat about 1 minute or until fragrant; cool. Combine spice mixture, butter and coriander in bowl; mix well.

Tomato Olive Butter: Combine all ingredients in bowl; mix well.

Serves 6.

- All butters can be rolled in foil, wrapped firmly and refrigerated or frozen for future use.
- Burgers can be prepared a day ahead. Butters can be prepared a week ahead.
- Storage: Covered, in refrigerator.
- Freeze: Suitable.
- Microwave: Not suitable.

CURRY SCONE ROLLS WITH MINT BUTTER

1 cup plain flour
1 cup self-raising flour
30g butter
150ml can coconut milk
½ cup water, approximately
2 tablespoons oil
30g butter, extra

FILLING
40g butter
3 teaspoons curry powder
1 teaspoon cumin seeds, crushed
4 green shallots, chopped
750g minced beef
2 tablespoons chutney
1 cup (70g) stale breadcrumbs

MINT BUTTER
125g butter
¼ cup chopped fresh mint

Sift flours into bowl, rub in butter. Stir in coconut milk and enough water to mix to a firm dough. Knead on lightly floured surface until smooth. Roll dough into a 22cm x 32cm rectangle. Spread filling evenly

over dough, roll up from long side like a Swiss roll, brush edges with water to seal. Refrigerate 15 minutes.

Cut roll into 2cm thick slices. Heat oil and extra butter on barbecue plate or in pan. Cook slices of roll in batches until browned on both sides. Serve slices with mint butter.

Filling: Heat butter in pan, add curry powder, seeds and shallots, cook, stirring, 1 minute. Remove from heat; cool. Combine shallot mixture, mince, chutney and breadcrumbs in bowl; mix well.

Mint Butter: Beat butter in small bowl with electric mixer until light and creamy, beat in mint.

Serves 6 to 8.

■ Filling and butter can be made 2 days ahead.
■ Storage: Covered, in refrigerator.
■ Freeze: Uncooked roll and butter suitable.
■ Microwave: Not suitable.

LEMON PATTIES

750g minced beef
2 cloves garlic, crushed
2 eggs, lightly beaten
2 teaspoons grated lemon rind
¼ cup grated parmesan cheese
½ cup stale breadcrumbs
2 tablespoons chopped fresh parsley

Combine all ingredients in bowl; mix well. Shape mixture into 8 patties. Barbecue or grill patties until cooked through.

Serves 4 to 6.

■ Patties can be prepared a day ahead.
■ Storage: Covered, in refrigerator.
■ Freeze: Suitable.
■ Microwave: Not suitable.

LEFT: Burgers with Assorted Butters: clockwise from back: Coriander Curry Butter, Tomato Olive Butter, Anchovy Butter, Mustard Butter.
ABOVE: From left: Lemon Patties, Curry Scone Rolls with Mint Butter.

Left: Pottery from Kenwick Galleries.

119

LAMB KOFTA WITH TOMATO SAUCE AND YOGURT

500g minced lamb
½ cup cracked wheat
1 onion, chopped
1 clove garlic, crushed
1 teaspoon ground coriander
1 teaspoon garam masala
2 tablespoons olive oil
2 pitta pocket breads
200g carton plain yogurt

TOMATO SAUCE
2 tablespoons olive oil
2 large (about 500g) tomatoes, peeled, chopped
1 teaspoon paprika
1 tablespoon chopped fresh coriander

Blend or process mince, wheat, onion, garlic, coriander and garam masala until combined. Shape 2 level tablespoons of mixture onto skewers.

Heat oil on barbecue plate or in pan, cook kofta until well browned and cooked through. Split pitta bread in half, toast on both sides until crisp. Top halves with kofta, tomato sauce and yogurt.

Tomato Sauce: Heat oil in pan, add tomatoes and paprika, cook, stirring, about 5 minutes or until sauce is thick, stir in coriander.

Serves 4.

- Kofta can be made a day ahead.
- Storage: Covered, in refrigerator.
- Freeze: Uncooked kofta suitable.
- Microwave: Not suitable.

LAMB AND CORN KEBABS

4 fresh corn cobs
500g minced lamb
1 teaspoon ground cumin
1 teaspoon ground coriander
2 tablespoons honey
1 tablespoon light soy sauce
2 teaspoons lemon juice
1 cup (70g) stale breadcrumbs
2 tablespoons chopped fresh parsley

Boil, steam or microwave corn until just tender; drain. Cut corn into 2cm rounds.

Process remaining ingredients until combined. Shape mixture into 16 patties. Thread corn and patties onto skewers, starting and finishing each skewer with corn; refrigerate 20 minutes.

Barbecue or grill kebabs until patties are cooked through.

Serves 4.

- Recipe can be prepared a day ahead.
- Storage: Covered, in refrigerator.
- Freeze: Uncooked patties suitable.
- Microwave: Corn suitable.

BARBECUED PITTA SANDWICH

700g minced lamb
¼ teaspoon cracked black peppercorns
2 cloves garlic, crushed
6 wholemeal pitta pocket breads
1 red Spanish onion, sliced
1¼ cups (125g) mozzarella cheese, grated
½ cup black olives, chopped
2 large (about 500g) tomatoes, sliced
1 tablespoon olive oil

Combine mince, pepper and garlic in bowl; mix well. Shape mixture into 12 patties. Barbecue or grill patties until browned and cooked through.

Open pocket in each pitta bread, fill with patties, onion, cheese, olives and tomatoes. Close pitta pockets, brush with oil, barbecue or grill until lightly browned and cheese is melted.

Serves 6.

- Patties can be prepared a day ahead.
- Storage: Covered, in refrigerator.
- Freeze: Uncooked patties suitable.
- Microwave: Not suitable.

Clockwise from front: Lamb Kofta with Tomato Sauce and Yogurt, Lamb and Corn Kebabs, Barbecued Pitta Sandwich.

CHICKEN AND BASIL SAUSAGES

500g minced chicken
2 cloves garlic, crushed
1 teaspoon chicken stock powder
2 small fresh red chillies, chopped
⅓ cup chopped fresh basil
2 eggs
½ cup coarsely grated fresh parmesan cheese
2 cups (200g) packaged breadcrumbs

CREAMY TOMATO SAUCE
1 large (about 250g) tomato, seeded, chopped
2 green shallots, chopped
¼ cup tomato sauce
3 teaspoons Worcestershire sauce
½ cup plain yogurt
½ cup sour cream

Blend or process mince, garlic, stock powder, chillies, basil, eggs, cheese and breadcrumbs until well combined and pasty. Shape level ¼ cups of mixture into balls, roll into thick sausage shapes. Barbecue or grill sausages until browned and cooked through. Serve with creamy tomato sauce.

Creamy Tomato Sauce: Combine all ingredients in bowl; mix well.

Serves 4.

- Sausages and sauce can be made separately a day ahead.
- Storage: Covered, in refrigerator.
- Freeze: Uncooked sausages suitable.
- Microwave: Not suitable.

COCONUT CHICKEN BURGERS WITH PAPAW MAYONNAISE

4 medium spinach (silverbeet) leaves, shredded
1 tablespoon oil
1 onion, finely chopped
1kg minced chicken
1 cup (70g) stale breadcrumbs
1 small chicken stock cube
1 egg, lightly beaten
plain flour
1 egg, extra
2 tablespoons milk
2 cups (140g) shredded coconut

PAPAW MAYONNAISE
2 egg yolks
½ teaspoon French mustard
½ teaspoon lemon juice
1½ teaspoons white vinegar
½ cup oil
3 teaspoons honey
¼ cup (about 100g) papaw pulp
½ cup thickened cream, whipped

Boil, steam or microwave spinach until just wilted; drain well, cool. Heat oil in pan, add onion, cook, stirring, until onion is soft; drain, cool.

Combine spinach, onion mixture, mince, breadcrumbs, crumbled stock cube and egg in bowl; mix well. Shape mixture into 8 patties.

Toss patties in flour, shake away excess flour, Dip patties in combined extra egg and milk, toss in coconut. Barbecue or grill patties over low heat until burgers are browned and cooked through. Serve with papaw mayonnaise.

Papaw Mayonnaise: Blend or process egg yolks, mustard, juice and vinegar until smooth. Add oil gradually in a thin stream while motor is operating; stir in honey and papaw pulp, fold in cream.

Serves 6 to 8.

- Recipe can be prepared a day ahead.
- Storage: Covered, in refrigerator.
- Freeze: Uncooked patties suitable.
- Microwave: Spinach suitable.

MEATBALL KEBABS WITH APRICOTS AND ZUCCHINI

300g minced pork and veal
1 small onion, chopped
2 teaspoons lime juice
½ teaspoon ground cardamom
½ teaspoon ground cinnamon
½ teaspoon ground coriander
½ cup stale breadcrumbs
1 egg white
1 tablespoon chopped fresh parsley
½ cup dried apricots
⅔ cup hot water
4 medium (about 400g) zucchini
1 tablespoon oil

YOGURT SAUCE
½ cup plain yogurt
2 tablespoons sour cream
1 tablespoon chopped fresh chives

Process mince, onion, juice, spices, breadcrumbs, egg white and parsley until combined. Roll level tablespoons of mixture into balls; cover, refrigerate 20 minutes. Combine apricots and water in bowl, cover, stand 20 minutes; drain. Cut zucchini into 1cm rounds. Thread zucchini, meatballs and apricots onto skewers. Brush with oil, barbecue or grill until cooked through. Serve kebabs with yogurt sauce.

Yogurt Sauce: Combine all ingredients in bowl; mix well.

Serves 4.

- Recipe can be prepared a day ahead.
- Storage: Covered, in refrigerator.
- Freeze: Uncooked meatballs suitable.
- Microwave: Not suitable.

CRUNCHY SATAY PATTIES

500g minced pork and veal
1 onion, chopped
1 egg, lightly beaten
½ cup stale breadcrumbs
⅓ cup milk
1½ cups (225g) chopped peanuts
1 tablespoon oil

SATAY SAUCE
1 tablespoon oil
1 onion, chopped
1 clove garlic, crushed
1 teaspoon sambal oelek
2 teaspoons curry powder
½ cup crunchy peanut butter
1 cup water
2 teaspoons light soy sauce
1 small chicken stock cube
150g can coconut milk
1 tablespoon lime juice
1 tablespoon chopped fresh
    coriander

Combine mince, onion, egg and breadcrumbs in bowl; mix well; shape into 8 patties. Dip in milk, toss in peanuts; press nuts on firmly. Heat oil on barbecue plate or in pan, add patties, cook until tender. Serve with satay sauce.

Satay Sauce: Heat oil in pan, add onion, garlic, sambal oelek and curry powder, cook, stirring, until onion is soft. Stir in peanut butter, water, sauce, crumbled stock cube, milk and juice; simmer, uncovered, about 5 minutes or until slightly thickened; stir in coriander.

Serves 4.

- Recipe can be prepared a day ahead.
- Storage: Covered, in refrigerator.
- Freeze: Uncooked patties suitable.
- Microwave: Sauce suitable.

LEFT: From top: Chicken and Basil Sausages, Coconut Chicken Burgers with Papaw Mayonnaise.
RIGHT: From top: Crunchy Satay Patties, Meatball Kebabs with Apricots and Zucchini.

Right: China from Wedgwood.

GLOSSARY

Here are some terms, names and alternatives to help everyone use and understand our recipes perfectly.

ALCOHOL: is optional but gives a particular flavour. Use fruit juice or water instead to make up the liquid content required.

ALLSPICE: pimento in ground form.

ALMONDS, FLAKED: sliced almonds.

ARROWROOT: used mostly for thickening. Cornflour can be used instead.

BACON RASHERS: bacon slices.

BAMBOO SHOOTS: the young tender shoots of bamboo plants, available in cans. Mainly used to add texture to food.

BARBECUE SAUCE: a spicy sauce available from supermarkets.

BEAN SPROUTS: we used alfalfa sprouts and mung bean sprouts; either can be used in our recipes.

BEEF, MINCED: ground beef.

BEETROOT: regular round beet.

BICARBONATE OF SODA: also known as baking soda.

BLACK BEANS, SALTED, PACKAGED: fermented, salted soy beans. Canned and dried black beans can be substituted. Drain and rinse canned variety, soak and rinse dried variety. Leftover beans can keep for months in an airtight container in the refrigerator. Mash the beans when cooking to release flavour.

BLACK BEAN SAUCE: made from fermented whole and crushed soy beans, water and wheat flour.

BREADCRUMBS:

Packaged dry: use fine packaged breadcrumbs.

Stale: use 1 or 2 day old white bread made into crumbs by grating, blending or processing.

BURGHUL: also known as cracked wheat and is wheat which has been cracked by boiling, then re-dried; mostly used in Middle Eastern cooking.

BUTTER: use salted or unsalted (also called sweet) butter; 125g is equal to 1 stick butter.

CHEESE:

Cream: also known as Philly.

Feta: is white or pale cream, with a soft to firm open texture and tangy salty taste.

Jarlsberg: a Norwegian cheese made from cows' milk, has large holes and a mild, nutty taste.

Light Blue: soft, creamy, sweet cheese with delicate blue veins.

Mozzarella: a fresh, semi-soft cheese with a delicate, clean, fresh curd taste; has a low melting point and stringy texture when it is heated.

Parmesan: sharp-tasting cheese used as a flavour accent. We prefer to use fresh parmesan cheese, although parmesan is available finely grated.

Ricotta: a fresh, unripened light curd cheese with a rich flavour.

Roquefort: a firm, blue-veined cheese with a rich and piquant taste.

Smoked: use a firm smoked cheese.

Tasty: use a firm, good-tasting cheddar.

CHICK PEAS: also known as garbanzos.

CHILLIES: are available in many different types and sizes. The small ones (birds' eye or bird peppers) are the hottest. Use tight rubber gloves when chopping fresh chillies as they can burn your skin.

Flakes, dried: are available at Asian food stores.

Powder: the Asian variety is the hottest and is made from ground chillies. It can be used as a substitute for fresh chillies in the proportion of ½ teaspoon ground chilli powder to 1 medium chopped chilli.

COCONUT: we used desiccated coconut unless otherwise specified.

Cream: available in cans and cartons in supermarkets and Asian stores; coconut milk can be substituted, although it is not as thick.

Milk: available in cans from supermarkets.

Shredded: thin strips of dried coconut.

CORIANDER: also known as cilantro and Chinese parsley and is essential to many south-east Asian cuisines. Its seeds are the main ingredient of curry powder. A strongly flavoured herb, use it sparingly until accustomed to the unique flavor. Available fresh, ground and in seed form.

CORNFLOUR: cornstarch.

CORNMEAL: ground corn (maize), similar to polenta but pale yellow and finer. One can be substituted for the other but results will be slightly different.

CRACKED WHEAT: see Burghul.

CREAM: light pouring cream, also known as half 'n' half.

Light Sour: a less dense, commercially cultured soured cream; do not substitute this for sour cream.

Sour: a thick, commercially cultured soured cream.

Thickened (whipping): is specified when necessary in recipes. Double cream or cream with more than 35 percent fat can be substituted.

CURRY POWDER: a convenient combination of spices in powdered form. It consists of chilli, coriander, cumin, fennel, fenugreek and turmeric in varying proportions.

EGG NOODLES, FRESH: made from wheat flour and eggs; varying in thickness from fine strands to pieces as thick as a shoelace.

EGG PASTRY SHEETS: spring roll, egg or gow gees pastry can be substituted.

EGGPLANT: aubergine.

FISH SAUCE: made from the liquid drained from salted, fermented anchovies. Has a strong smell and taste; use sparingly.

FIVE SPICE POWDER: a pungent mixture of ground spices which includes cinnamon, cloves, fennel, star anise and Szechwan peppers.

FLOUR:

Plain (white): all-purpose flour.

Rice: flour made from rice; ground rice can be substituted.

Self-raising: substitute plain (all-purpose) flour and baking powder in the proportion of ¾ metric cup plain flour to 2 level metric teaspoons of baking powder. Sift together several times before using. If using 8oz imperial measuring cup, use 1 cup plain flour to 2 teaspoons baking powder.

Wholemeal plain: wholewheat flour without the addition of baking powder.

GARAM MASALA: varied combinations of cardamom, cinnamon, cloves, coriander, cumin and nutmeg make this spice which is often used in Indian cooking. Sometimes pepper is used to make a hot variation.

GARBANZOS: canned chick peas.

GARLIC: can be used crushed, sliced or whole cloves; a bulb contains many cloves.

GHERKIN: cornichon.

GINGER:

Fresh, Green or Root Ginger: scrape away outside skin and grate, chop or slice ginger as required. To preserve fresh, peeled ginger, cover with enough dry sherry in a jar and refrigerate. It will keep for months.

Ground: is available but should not be substituted for fresh ginger.

GOW GEES PASTRY: wonton wrappers, spring roll or egg pastry sheets can be substituted.

GREEN PEPPERCORNS: available in cans or jars, pickled in brine.

GREEN SHALLOTS: also known as scallions and spring onions. Do not confuse with the small golden shallots.

HERBS: we have specified when to use fresh or dried herbs. We used dried (not ground) herbs in the proportion of 1:4 for fresh herbs, for example, 1 teaspoon dried herbs instead of 4 teaspoons (1 tablespoon) chopped fresh herbs.

HOI SIN SAUCE: is a thick sweet Chinese barbecue sauce made from a mixture of salted black beans, onion and garlic.

HORSERADISH CREAM: paste of horseradish, oil, mustard and flavourings.

HUMMUS: a paste of chick peas, tahini, garlic, lemon juice and olive oil.

JALAPENO PEPPERS: imported, canned, pickled, hot chillies. Store leftover chillies in their liquid in an airtight container in the refrigerator.

JUNIPER BERRIES: dried berries of an evergreen tree; it is the main flavouring ingredient in gin.

KUMARA: an orange-coloured sweet potato.

LARD: fat obtained from melting down and clarifying pork fat; available packaged.

LEEK: a member of the onion family, resembles the green shallot but is much larger.

MIRIN: a sweet rice wine used in Japanese cooking. Substitute 1 teaspoon sugar and 1 teaspoon dry sherry for each tablespoon mirin.

MIXED SPICE: a blend of ground spices usually consisting of cinnamon, allspice and nutmeg.

MORTADELLA: a delicately spiced and smoked cooked sausage made of pork and beef.

MUSHROOMS:

Baby: small, unopened mushrooms with a delicate flavour.

Dried Chinese: have a unique flavour. Place mushrooms in bowl, cover with boiling water, stand 20 minutes; drain mushrooms, discard stems, use caps as indicated in recipes.

Flat: large, soft, flat mushrooms with a rich strong flavour.

MUSHROOM SUPREME: canned baby mushrooms with milk, cream, cheese, onions and bacon.

MUSTARD:

Dry: available in powder form.

Seeded: a French-style mustard with crushed mustard seeds.

OIL: polyunsaturated vegetable oil.

Olive: virgin oil is obtained only from the pulp of high-grade fruit. Pure olive oil is pressed from the pulp and kernels of second grade olives. Extra virgin olive oil is the purest quality virgin oil.

OYSTER SAUCE: a rich brown sauce made from oysters cooked in salt and soy sauce, then thickened with starches.

PARSLEY, FLAT-LEAFED: also known as continental parsley or Italian parsley.

PEPPERONI: sausage made from minced pork and beef with added fat. Flavoured with ground hot red pepper.

PEPPERS: capsicum or bell peppers.

PIMIENTOS: canned or bottled peppers.

PLUM SAUCE: a dipping sauce which consists of plums preserved in vinegar, sweetened with sugar and flavoured with chillies and spices.

POLENTA: usually made from ground corn (maize); similar to cornmeal but coarser and darker in colour. One can be substituted for the other but results will be slightly different.

PRAWNS: shrimp.

PROSCIUTTO: uncooked, unsmoked ham, cured in salt, ready to eat when bought.

PRUNES: whole dried plums with a dark, wrinkled appearance.

READY-ROLLED PUFF PASTRY: frozen sheets of puff pastry available from supermarkets.

RED SPANISH ONION: large purplish-red onion.

RICE, WILD: from North America, but not a member of the rice family. It is expensive and difficult to cultivate but has a distinctive flavour.

RIND: zest.

SAFFRON: available in strands or ground form, made from the dried stamens of the crocus flower. The quality varies greatly.

SAMBAL OELEK: a paste made from ground chillies and salt.

SEASONED PEPPER: a combination of pepper, red pepper, garlic flakes, paprika and natural chicken extract.

SESAME OIL: made from roasted, crushed white sesame seeds and always used in small quantities. Do not use for deep-frying.

SESAME SEEDS: there are 2 types, black and white; we used the white variety in this book. To toast: spread seeds evenly onto oven tray, toast in moderate oven for about 5 minutes.

SNOW PEAS: also known as *mange tout* (eat all), sugar peas or Chinese peas.

SOY SAUCE: made from fermented soy beans. The light sauce is generally used with white meat, and the darker variety with red meat. There is a multi-purpose salt-reduced sauce available, also Japanese soy sauce. It is personal taste which sauce you use.

SPINACH, ENGLISH: a soft-leaved vegetable, more delicate in taste than silverbeet (spinach); however, young silverbeet can be substituted for English spinach.

SPINACH (silverbeet): remove coarse white stems, cook green leafy parts as required by recipes.

SPRING ONIONS: vegetables with small white bulbs and long green leaves.

SPRING ROLL PASTRY SHEETS: wonton wrappers, gow gee or egg pastry sheets can be substituted.

STAR ANISE: the dried star-shaped fruit of an evergreen tree. It is used sparingly in Chinese cooking and has an aniseed flavour.

STOCK: home-made stock can be used in our recipes in place of stock cube, powder and water, if preferred. Condensed stock in cartons is also available.

Cubes: beef, chicken or vegetable flavours available.

Powder: 1 teaspoon stock powder is roughly equivalent to 1 small stock cube.

SUGAR: We used coarse granulated table sugar, also known as crystal sugar, unless otherwise specified.

Brown: a soft finely granulated sugar with molasses present which gives it its characteristic colour.

Castor: fine granulated table sugar.

SUET: the hard, white fat that surrounds the kidney in beef and mutton. Available from the butcher. 300g fresh suet will give about 2 cups (150g) grated fresh suet.

SULTANAS: seedless white raisins.

TABASCO SAUCE: made with vinegar, hot red peppers and salt. Use sparingly.

TAHINI PASTE: made from crushed sesame seeds.

TOMATO:

Paste: a concentrated tomato puree used in flavouring soups, stews, sauces, etc.

Puree: is canned, pureed tomatoes (not tomato paste). Use fresh, peeled, pureed tomatoes as a substitute, if preferred.

Sun-dried: are dried tomatoes sometimes bottled in oil.

TOMATO SAUCE: tomato ketchup.

TOMATO SUPREME: a canned product consisting of tomatoes, onions, celery, peppers and seasonings.

VEGEMITE: yeast extract spread. Marmite or Promite can be substituted.

VINEGAR: both white and brown (malt) vinegar are used in this book.

Balsamic: originated in the province of Modena, Italy. Regional wine is specially processed then aged in antique wooden casks to give a pungent flavour.

Cider: vinegar made from fermented apples.

Rice: a colourless, seasoned vinegar containing sugar and salt.

Tarragon White Wine: made from wine, flavoured with tarragon.

WATER CHESTNUTS: small white crisp bulbs with a brown skin. Canned water chestnuts are peeled and will keep for about a month in the refrigerator.

WINE: we used good quality dry white and red wines.

WITLOF: also known as chicory or Belgian endive.

WONTON WRAPPERS: gow gee, egg or spring roll pastry sheets can be substituted.

WORCESTERSHIRE SAUCE: is a spicy sauce used mainly on red meat.

YEAST: allow 2 teaspoons (7g) dried granulated yeast to each 15g compressed yeast if substituting one for the other.

ZUCCHINI: courgette.

INDEX

Cup and Spoon Measurements

To ensure accuracy in your recipes use the standard metric measuring equipment approved by Standards Australia:
(a) 250 millilitre cup for measuring liquids. A litre jug *(capacity 4 cups)* is also available.
(b) a graduated set of four cups – measuring 1 cup, half, third and quarter cup – for items such as flour, sugar, etc. When measuring in these fractional cups, level off at the brim.
(c) a graduated set of four spoons: tablespoon *(20 millilitre liquid capacity)*, teaspoon *(5 millilitre)*, half and quarter teaspoons. The Australian, British and American teaspoon each has 5ml capacity.

Approximate cup and spoon conversion chart

Australian	American & British
1 cup	1¼ cups
¾ cup	1 cup
⅔ cup	¾ cup
½ cup	⅔ cup
⅓ cup	½ cup
¼ cup	⅓ cup
2 tablespoons	¼ cup
1 tablespoon	4 teaspoons

ALL SPOON MEASUREMENTS
ARE LEVEL.
Note: NZ, Canada, USA and UK all
use 15ml tablespoons.

Oven Temperatures

Electric	C°	F°
Very slow	120	250
Slow	150	300
Moderately slow	160-180	325-350
Moderate	180-200	375-400
Moderately hot	210-230	425-450
Hot	240-250	475-500
Very hot	260	525-550

Gas	C°	F°
Very slow	120	250
Slow	150	300
Moderately slow	160	325
Moderate	180	350
Moderately hot	190	375
Hot	200	400
Very hot	230	450

We have used large eggs
with an average weight of 60g each
in all recipes.

TWO GREAT OFFERS FROM THE AWW HOME LIBRARY

SHELVING YOUR INVESTMENTS

Here's the perfect way to keep your Home Library books in order, clean and within easy reach. More than a dozen books fit into this smart silver grey vinyl holder.

Phone now for your Home Library Holder
Yours for just $A9.95 each
(including postage and handling)

☎ Sydney (02) 260 0035
Elsewhere (in Australia) 008 252 515 (free call)
Have your credit card details ready (Mon - Fri, 9am - 5pm)
or Fax your details to Sydney (02) 282 8254
or write to AWW Home Library
GPO Box 7036 Sydney NSW 2001

Please allow up to 21 days for delivery within Australia. Overseas residents, please add $A10 per holder for postage. **OFFER VALID WHILE STOCKS LAST.**

HLMH91

AWW HOME LIBRARY OFFER

This durable set of cups and spoons has been made to accurately measure the ingredients called for in Home Library cookbook recipes.

PRICE : Australia: $5.95; New Zealand: $A8.00; elsewhere: $A9.95;
prices include postage & handling.

This offer is available in all countries.

TO ORDER YOUR METRIC MEASURING SET:
PHONE: Sydney (02) 260 0035; Elsewhere in Australia: 008 252 515
(free call) or FAX your order to (02) 267 4363 or MAIL your order by photocopying
or cutting out and completing the coupon below.
PAYMENT: **Australian residents:** We accept the credit cards listed, money orders and cheques. **Overseas residents:** We accept the credit cards listed, drafts in $A drawn on an Australian bank, also English, Canadian, New Zealand and U.S. cheques in the currency of the country of issue.
Credit card charges are at the exchange rate current at the time of payment.

Please photocopy and complete the coupon and forward to, or write to: AWW Home Library Reader Offer, ACP Direct PO Box 7036 Sydney 2001

Mr/Mrs/Ms _____
Address _____
_____
Postcode _____ Country _____
Ph: ( )_____ Bus. Hours _____
I enclose my cheque/money order for $ _____ payable to ACP Direct
Offer expires 31/12/92

OR: please charge my:
❏ Bankcard ❏ Visa ❏ MasterCard ❏ Diners Club ❏ Amex
[ ][ ][ ][ ][ ][ ][ ][ ][ ][ ][ ][ ][ ][ ][ ][ ] Exp. Date ___/__
Cardholder's signature_____

(Please allow up to 30 days for delivery within Australia. Allow up to 6 weeks for overseas deliveries.)

HLAW991